READINGS ON

THE SUN
ALSO RISES

OTHER TITLES IN THE GREENHAVEN PRESS LITERARY COMPANION SERIES:

AMERICAN AUTHORS

Maya Angelou
Stephen Crane
Emily Dickinson
William Faulkner
F. Scott Fitzgerald
Robert Frost
Nathaniel Hawthorne
Ernest Hemingway
Arthur Miller
Flannery O'Connor
Eugene O'Neill
Edgar Allan Poe
John Steinbeck
Mark Twain
Walt Whitman
Thornton Wilder

AMERICAN LITERATURE

The Adventures of Huckleberry Finn
The Adventures of Tom Sawyer
All My Sons
Black Boy
The Call of the Wild
The Catcher in the Rye
The Crucible
Death of a Salesman
Ethan Frome
Fahrenheit 451
A Farewell to Arms
The Glass Menagerie
The Grapes of Wrath
The Great Gatsby
Hard Times
Metamorphosis
My Ántonia
Native Son
Of Mice and Men
The Old Man and the Sea
One Flew Over the Cuckoo's Nest
Our Town
The Pearl
A Raisin in the Sun
The Red Pony
The Scarlet Letter
A Separate Peace
The Short Stories of Edgar Allan Poe
To Kill a Mockingbird
Twelve Angry Men
West Side Story

THE GREENHAVEN PRESS
Literary Companion
TO AMERICAN LITERATURE

READINGS ON

THE SUN ALSO RISES

Kelly Wand, *Book Editor*

Daniel Leone, *President*
Bonnie Szumski, *Publisher*
Scott Barbour, *Managing Editor*

Greenhaven Press, Inc., San Diego, CA

Every effort has been made to trace the owners of copy-righted material. The articles in this volume may have been edited for content, length, and/or reading level. The titles have been changed to enhance the editorial purpose. Those interested in locating the original source will find the complete citation on the first page of each article.

Library of Congress Cataloging-in-Publication Data

Readings on The sun also rises / Kelly Wand, book editor.
    p. cm. — (The Greenhaven Press literary
companion to American literature)
    Includes bibliographical references (p.) and index.
    ISBN 0-7377-0195-1 (lib. bdg. : alk. paper) —
ISBN 0-7377-0194-3 (pbk. : alk. paper)
    1. Hemingway, Ernest, 1899–1961. Sun also rises.
I. Wand, Kelly. II. Series.

PS3515.E37 S92   2002
813'.52—dc21   2001033796
                                                        CIP

Cover photo: Hulton-Deutsch/Corbis

"The chief criticism [of The Sun Also Rises] *seems to be that the people are so unattractive—which seems very funny as criticism when you consider the attractiveness of the people in, say,* Ulysses, *the Old Testament, Judge [Henry] Fielding and other people some of the critics like. I wonder where these thoroughly attractive people hang out and how they behave when they're drunk and what do* they *think about nights."*

—Ernest Hemingway, *Selected Letters*

CONTENTS

Chapter 1: Settings in *The Sun Also Rises*

Chapter 2: Characters in *The Sun Also Rises*

others also resent Cohn's prewar notions of romantic idealism.

Chapter 3: Themes in *The Sun Also Rises*

FOREWORD

*"'Tis the good reader that
makes the good book."*

Ralph Waldo Emerson

The story's bare facts are simple: The captain, an old and
scarred seafarer, walks with a peg leg made of whale ivory.
He relentlessly drives his crew to hunt the world's oceans for
the great white whale that crippled him. After a long search,
the ship encounters the whale and a fierce battle ensues. Finally the captain drives his harpoon into the whale, but the
harpoon line catches the captain about the neck and drags
him to his death.

A simple story, a straightforward plot—yet, since the 1851
publication of Herman Melville's *Moby-Dick*, readers and
critics have found many meanings in the struggle between
Captain Ahab and the whale. To some, the novel is a cau-
tionary tale that depicts how Ahab's obsession with revenge
leads to his insanity and death. Others believe that the whale
represents the unknowable secrets of the universe and that
Ahab is a tragic hero who dares to challenge fate by attempting to discover this knowledge. Perhaps Melville intended Ahab as a criticism of Americans' tendency to become involved in well-intentioned but irrational causes. Or
did Melville model Ahab after himself, letting his fictional
character express his anger at what he perceived as a cruel
and distant god?

Although literary critics disagree over the meaning of
Moby-Dick, readers do not need to choose one particular interpretation in order to gain an understanding of Melville's
novel. Instead, by examining various analyses, they can gain

numerous insights into the issues that lie under the surface of the basic plot. Studying the writings of literary critics can also aid readers in making their own assessments of *Moby-Dick* and other literary works and in developing analytical thinking skills.

The Greenhaven Literary Companion Series was created with these goals in mind. Designed for young adults, this unique anthology series provides an engaging and comprehensive introduction to literary analysis and criticism. The essays included in the Literary Companion Series are chosen for their accessibility to a young adult audience and are expertly edited in consideration of both the reading and comprehension levels of this audience. In addition, each essay is introduced by a concise summation that presents the contributing writer's main themes and insights. Every anthology in the Literary Companion Series contains a varied selection of critical essays that cover a wide time span and express diverse views. Wherever possible, primary sources are represented through excerpts from authors' notebooks, letters, and journals and through contemporary criticism.

Each title in the Literary Companion Series pays careful consideration to the historical context of the particular author or literary work. In-depth biographies and detailed chronologies reveal important aspects of authors' lives and emphasize the historical events and social milieu that influenced their writings. To facilitate further research, every anthology includes primary and secondary source bibliographies of articles and/or books selected for their suitability for young adults. These engaging features make the Greenhaven Literary Companion Series ideal for introducing students to literary analysis in the classroom or as a library resource for young adults researching the world's great authors and literature.

Exceptional in its focus on young adults, the Greenhaven Literary Companion Series strives to present literary criticism in a compelling and accessible format. Every title in the series is intended to spark readers' interest in leading American and world authors, to help them broaden their understanding of literature, and to encourage them to formulate their own analyses of the literary works that they read. It is the editors' hope that young adult readers will find these anthologies to be true companions in their study of literature.

INTRODUCTION

In July 1925, the promising young writer-poet Ernest Hemingway took his wife and some friends to the annual fiesta of bullfighting and hard-drinking revelry in Pamplona, Spain. Unlike previous expeditions, this one was a series of disasters. Ernest's cherished fishing spot had become a dusty swamp from logging operations. Petty hostilities and sexual resentments within the group caused lasting rifts. Everyone was relieved when it was over, especially Ernest, who within a week had already begun work on his first novel based on the Pamplona debacle.

The opening scene he quickly produced was a rather stagy third-person account of a young bullfighter named Pedro Romero being introduced by an innkeeper to two bullfighting "admirers" from America. Hemingway finished the draft a few months later in Paris, then, in Austria, began exhaustively revising it. He later referred to this as the "most difficult job of rewriting I have ever done."[1]

The novel was, of course, *The Sun Also Rises,* and after it was first published in 1926, nothing was ever the same. Hemingway became an international celebrity overnight. The book's critical and commercial success, his first of many, coronated him as spokesman for his generation and the undisputed reigning prince of modernism. The book was especially popular among the young. Boys on college campuses everywhere talked and acted like the novel's world-weary narrator Jake Barnes, while the girls adopted Brett Ashleyisms, including her bob haircut. The reviewer in the *New York Times Book Review* called it "magnificent writing, filled with that organic action which gives a compelling picture of character."[2] With just one book, Hemingway had fathered an entirely new style, the art of storytelling through deliberate omission. Many years later, he compared *The Sun Also Rises* to an iceberg, where the invisible seven-eighths under the surface provides massive support for the top that shows. Though he went on to write numerous other critically praised best-sellers and eventually win the Nobel and Pulitzer Prizes for his "powerful, style-making mastery of the art of modern narration,"[3] *The Sun Also Rises* never ceased to be the only novel he looked back on with complete satisfaction in his own prowess.

Though Hemingway scorned literary criticism all his life, more has been written about his slender first novel than any other American writer's entire canon (with the possible exception of Mark Twain). Arguments still rage between scholars to this day over whether the ending is happy or sad, whether Brett Ashley is evil or just misunderstood, even over the meaning of the title. What they do all agree on is that Hemingway was a masterful writer. In his case, characterization, setting, and subtext are all so painstakingly interwoven that isolating a single aspect is extremely difficult. So, though rather loosely classified under such headings as "setting" and "theme," selections in this volume examine the variety of overlapping methods Hemingway used—his real life experiences in France and Spain, his considerable craft in prose, and his insight into the emotions which rule all human beings—to create the work of fiction that would immortalize him, *The Sun Also Rises*.

NOTES

1. Quoted in Frederic Joseph Svoboda, *Hemingway and* The Sun Also Rises: *The Crafting of a Style.* Lawrence: University Press of Kansas, 1983, p. 23.

2. *New York Times Book Review*, October 31, 1926, p. 7.

3. Quoted in Carlos Baker, *Ernest Hemingway: A Life Story.* New York: Charles Scribner's Sons, 1969, p. 528.

ERNEST HEMINGWAY: A BIOGRAPHY

On July 21, 1899, Ernest Miller Hemingway was born in his family's home at 439 Oak Park Avenue in the town of the same name. Oak Park, Illinois, was a conservative upper-middle-class suburb Hemingway would later refer to as a township of "wide lawns and narrow minds."[1] Ernest was the second of six children born to Clarence Edmonds and Grace Hall Hemingway, who named their son after Grace's father, Ernest Hall, and his great uncle Miller Hall. Clarence, a doctor who was known to his friends as Ed, was the eldest son of Anson T. Hemingway, a Civil War veteran. Ed was an outdoorsman of considerable fortitude; he fished, hunted, cooked, and performed amateur taxidermy as well as collecting Pottawatomi Indian arrowheads and snakes, which he kept preserved in sealed glass jars of alcohol. He had first encountered Hemingway's mother, Grace Hall, when they were both high school students. Grace taught music at home for the five years following her graduation. Her poor eyesight thwarted her dreams, supported by her mother and teachers, to become a professional opera singer. After their wedding, they moved in with Grace's widowed father, Ernest Hall, a war veteran like Anson who ran a successful cutlery business in Chicago and handled the bulk of the newlyweds' bills.

Like the rest of Oak Park's deeply religious residents, the senior Hemingways held dear the Midwestern Protestant work ethic and raised their children accordingly. Work hard, worship God, and stay fit, Ernest was told early on, and you will prosper. While his father taught him to hunt and fish and appreciate the tranquility of nature, his mother stressed an interest in the arts and insisted Ernest practice the cello. Despite this well-rounded education, nothing in his youth presaged Ernest's meteoric rise to literary prominence and worldwide celebrity.

GROWING UP HEMINGWAY

Hemingway took more after his father early on, preferring squirrel hunting in the woods near Windemere, the family's summer house on Walloon Lake in northern Michigan, to his mother's cello lessons and choir practices. According to biographer Carlos Baker, "He shared his father's determination to do things 'properly' (a favorite adverb in both their vocabularies), whether building a fire, rigging a rod, baiting a hook, casting a fly, handling a gun, or roasting a duck or a haunch of venison."[2] These early experiences with nature would influence Hemingway and his writing for the rest of his life. Though his twenties were spent in major cities like Paris and Chicago, once he was successful he chose remote places to live like Ketchum, Idaho, or Key West, Florida, anywhere with some kind of wild game. Nature also proved to be an abiding force in his lifetime of writing, while music did not (though his mother's influence at least helped him later break the ice with his first wife, Hadley, an aspiring pianist).

Hemingway, who would one day receive both Nobel and Pultizer Prizes for redefining the English language, was a product of the public school system. He was mediocre at high school sports (which included track, football, and water basketball) but enjoyed writing funny pieces for the newspaper, the *Trapeze* (his writing model was popular satirist Ring Lardner, who wrote an acclaimed column in the *Chicago Tribune*). After graduating in 1917, his parents were crushed by his decision to forgo college and instead take a job as a cub reporter for the *Kansas City Star*, one of the leading papers of its day. He secured this job through his Uncle Tyler, who knew the paper's chief editorial columnist. No stranger to rigid discipline, Hemingway was quick to take to a prose style stripped bare of all but the cold, hard facts and would later look back on this literary boot camp with awe and gratitude.

THE GREAT WAR

Within weeks of Hemingway's high school graduation, America became involved in a war the scope of which the world had never seen. The United States joined the Allies to battle the forces of Germany and Austria in April 1917. When he turned eighteen, Hemingway tried to enlist but was turned down because of his poor vision, which ran in the family on his mother's side. The Red Cross was less picky and accepted him as an ambulance driver in December 1917. The following April he left the *Star*, and in May he was on a ship for Europe. "I was an awful dope when I went to the last war," Hemingway recollected in 1942. "I can remember just thinking that we were the home team and the Austrians were the visiting team."[3]

After a brief stopover in Paris, he traveled to Milan, Italy, in early June. On the day of his arrival, a munitions factory exploded, and he spent his first hours off the train carrying mutilated bodies and body parts to a makeshift morgue. Two days later he was sent to the town of Schio to drive ambulances. Only a few weeks later, on July 8, 1918, Hemingway was sent to deliver chocolate and cigarettes to Italian soldiers in the trenches at the front along the Piave River. While he was there, an Austrian mortar shell exploded within a few feet of him, knocking him unconscious, killing one Italian soldier, and blowing the legs off another. With more than two hundred pieces of shrapnel embedded in his legs, Hemingway still managed to carry a wounded soldier back to the first aid station, along the way taking a machine-gun bullet in one leg. Later, speaking at an assembly at his old high school, he referred to the event:

> Just before we reached the trench their searchlight spotted us and they turned a machine gun on us. One got me in the thigh. It felt just like a snowball. . . . It knocked me down. We started on, but just as we reached the trench and were about to jump in, another bullet hit me, this time in the foot. It tumbled me and my wounded man all in a heap in the trench and when I came to again I was in a dugout. Two soldiers had just come to the conclusion that I was to "pass out shortly." By some arguing I was able to convince them they were wrong.[4]

Hemingway was awarded the Italian Silver Medal for Valor. His subsequent recovery in a hospital in Milan, where he fell in love with his nurse Agnes von Kurowsky (who later rejected him as too young for her), would later become the basis for two novels, *A Farewell to Arms* and, to a lesser extent, *The Sun Also Rises*.

HOMECOMING

When he returned to the United States in January 1919, Hemingway felt an extremely old nineteen and a half but basked in the glow of being considered a hometown war hero. He was asked to speak about his exploits at his old high school and to local papers, which led to a variety of local speaking engagements. Despite this status and the increased confidence it gave him, his parents were not pleased. Hemingway had been able to avoid work for nearly a year because of the thousand dollars he received in insurance payments for his war wounds, and he spent much of his time at home reading. His parents called him to task for not thinking enough about his future and issued him an ultimatum to either find work immediately or begin earning a degree. Hemingway was eager not just to find employment but also to move out.

One of Hemingway's speaking engagements was at the Petoskey Public Library. One of the listeners there, Harriett Connable, was so impressed by his vigor, she offered him a job as a tutor for her frail, introverted son. Hemingway accepted the position, his decision abetted by the prospect of an introduction to the editor of the *Toronto Star Weekly* by Harriet's husband Ralph. He began writing freelance articles for the *Star Weekly* in early 1920.

PARIS'S "LOST GENERATION"

In the fall of 1920, Hemingway moved to Chicago but continued writing for the *Star Weekly*. While staying with a friend there, he met Hadley Richardson. They immediately fell in love and married in September 1921. That November, Hemingway agreed to go to Paris and serve as the European correspondent for the *Toronto Daily Star*. Paris was already a haven for American artist expatriates. The living was also incredibly cheap, and, better yet, alcoholic beverages were legal in France, as opposed to the United States, where Prohibition was in effect. Hemingway had already become a hard drinker and spoke highly of the creative connections inspired by intoxication, though he scorned doing any actual writing while under the influence.

The Hemingways moved into their first apartment in Paris just before Christmas 1921. It was a dilapidated place with no running water and a bathroom that consisted of a closet containing a slop bucket. Hemingway's enthusiasm for the bohemian lifestyle buoyed Hadley's spirits. He rented a separate room where he could write in peace, and the two settled in.

Hemingway plunged enthusiastically into Parisian social life. Using a letter of introduction from writer Sherwood Anderson, he befriended a circle of prominent artists, including other American "expatriates" such as Ezra Pound and Gertrude Stein. Stein coined the phrase "the lost generation," which would come to embody everyone of Hemingway's age whom the Great War had displaced or somehow scarred (interestingly, Stein herself had acquired the term from a garage owner in a remote French village in reference to his untrainable group of young car mechanics). Knowing so many of the century's greatest artistic minds understandably set Hemingway's creative juices flowing, but for his first two years in France, most of his writing was news reporting for the *Toronto Star Weekly*. Along with covering the Greco-Turkish War and the Geneva Conference in 1922, he also wrote sports articles on bullfighting, fishing, skiing, and bobsledding.

A Promising Young Scribe

When Hadley discovered she was pregnant, she expressed her preference for American doctors and hospitals. The Hemingways left France in 1923 and moved to Toronto, Ohio, where Ernest continued to write for the *Star*. On October 10, their son John Hadley Nicanor Hemingway was born, and by January 1924, they were on their way back to Paris, where Hemingway could resume his career with zeal.

At Ezra Pound's endorsement, the successful writer and editor Ford Maddox Ford took Hemingway on to edit his new literary magazine, the *Transatlantic Review*. "He's an experienced journalist," Pound wrote to Ford. "He writes very good verse and he's the finest prose stylist in the world."[5] The *Review*, though regarded as a respectable journal, was defunct after only a year and a half, but several of Hemingway's first stories appeared there, including "Indian Camp" and "Cross Country Snow." His first collection of short fiction, *Three Stories and Ten Poems*, was published in 1923. A year later he published *in our time*, a series of short sketches, which was published in 1925, expanded and revised, as *In Our Time*. Already, Hemingway's fiction followed the dictum he later made famous: that fewer words, when the right ones, enhanced drama. He illustrated his theory with the image of an iceberg with only the top eighth visible. The rest is there but "submerged" between the lines. He followed up the collection with *Torrents of Spring*, a barbed satire on his former mentor Sherwood Anderson. (F. Scott Fitzgerald called *Torrents of Spring* "the finest comic novel ever written by an American."[6])

THE SUN ALSO RISES

In July 1925, the Hemingways traveled to Pamplona for its annual fiesta with the witty Donald Ogden Stewart and a Michigan fishing friend named Bill Smith. Lady Duff Twysden and Harold Loeb, the first Jewish student admitted to Princeton, met them there after their stay at the coastal resort of St. Jean-de-Luz. Lady Duff's husband-to-be, a drunken Scotsman named Pat Guthrie, also joined them, and together they enjoyed the wizardry of Cayetano Ordonez in the bullfighting ring. Fighting under the name Nino de la Palma, the bullfighter later presented Hadley with the ear of a bull, which she left in the drawer of her room at the hotel.

The trip was a fiasco. Ernest, Hadley, and Bill went to fish the Irati the week prior to the fiesta and found it befouled by logging operations. "Fish killed, pools destroyed, dams broken down," said Ernest. "Made me feel sick."[7] Then, in Pamplona, Hemingway and Loeb nearly came to blows in the street. Though Hadley was in attendance for the duration of the trip, it was clear that Hemingway was quite taken with Lady Twysden and seething with resentment over her having gone off with Loeb for a temporary romance at St. Jean-de-Luz in June. Added to the catalogue of offenses was Loeb's daredevil move while running with the bulls in the streets of Pamplona: "Harold, resplendent in a Fair Isle sweater, seized the horns of one of the bulls. He held his white sneakers aloft like an acrobat, and was borne rapidly across the field of combat, his horn-rimmed glasses still in place, out-Hemingwaying Hemingway."[8]

Hemingway's account of the following night, according to Baker, revealed that sexual tensions among the traveling companions had reached the boiling point:

> Harold and Duff had slipped away from the others for a drink in one of the cafes. Their small carouse had ended in a Spanish clubroom in one of the buildings on the square, where Duff, as the only woman, was like the queen bee in a hive of drones. She refused to leave, and Harold was obliged to return to the hotel alone. She appeared for lunch with a black eye and a contusion on her forehead. When Harold asked about it, Ernest cut him short by saying that she had fallen against a railing. "Pat was sour, ugly. Hadley had lost her smile. Don tried a quip that went lame. Bill looked grim." Over the brandy that night, Guthrie suddenly told Harold to get out; he was not wanted. Harold turned to Duff, who said at once that she did not want him to go. Ernest exploded in

manly wrath. "You lousy bastard," he shouted at Loeb, "running to a woman."[9]

Loeb asked Hemingway to step outside, but once there, they both admitted neither wanted to hit the other. Though the next day Hemingway wrote Loeb a note apologizing for his "meanness" and stating that he was "thoroughly ashamed," friendships within the group never recovered.

Following the festival, Hemingway stayed in Spain and began writing his first novel, which he originally planned to title *Fiesta,* based on these events. In the early drafts, the bullfighter was the main protagonist. Hemingway changed the names of the rest of the group, fiddled extensively with their personalities, and, after much thought, changed his own "character," Jake Barnes, into a man who'd been left impotent from war injuries. After further tinkering in Paris, he altered the opening to focus on Lady Brett Ashley (the Duff character) so that the first two chapters were concerned entirely with her background. The final draft was completed on September 21, 1925, exactly two months after his twenty-sixth birthday. Over the winter in Schruns, Austria, he revised the novel further and sent it off to Scribner's in New York City. F. Scott Fitzgerald, his friend and rival, urged him to cut the opening two chapters on Brett's background, claiming the tone was too arch and "shop-worn." Hemingway took this advice and on October 22, 1926, the novel was published at a price of two dollars, changing his life forever. *The Sun Also Rises* was a critical and commercial smash.

Naturally, many of the real-life characters he had portrayed in the novel were less than thrilled with their representation. Loeb was understandably shattered. Duff, the inspiration for Brett Ashley, was enraged at first, but eventually "her only quibble was that she had not in fact slept with the bloody bullfighter."[10]

A NEW WIFE IN KEY WEST

Hemingway was at the height of his creative powers for the last half of the 1920s. But as his fame and literary light exploded, life at home deteriorated. In 1927 he divorced Hadley and married Pauline Pfeiffer, a fashion reporter for *Vanity Fair* and *Vogue.* The next year they left Paris for Key West, Florida, where the sport of game fishing would occupy Hemingway and influence his writing for more than a decade. Then, in December, word came by cable of his father's suicide by gunshot wound. Clarence Hemingway had suffered from a number of ailments, including diabetes and angina, and his mental state had deteriorated, little helped by speculative real estate purchases in Florida that had gone sour. Hemingway left immediately for Oak Park to oversee the funeral.

Despite this gloomy incident, Hemingway loved Key West. He called it "the best place I've ever been anytime, anywhere."[11] On June 28, 1928, Pauline gave birth to their son Patrick by cesarean section. Despite the loss of his father and the birth of his son, Hemingway's energy was concentrated on a new novel, which he finished in January 1929. *A Farewell to Arms* was published on September 27 to great acclaim and popularity. Gregory, the last of Hemingway's children and second son by Pauline, was born in 1931. The next year, Hemingway published his nonfictional treatise on Spanish bullfighting, *Death in the Afternoon.* Its theme was "grace under pressure," such as that demonstrated by Pedro Romero in *The Sun Also Rises.* Hemingway was quite taken with stoic heroes who looked death in the eye while they finessed a deadly enemy into the dirt, but this time critics accused him of sounding blustery and of having repeated himself poorly.

Returning to fiction in 1933, Hemingway released another short story collection, *Winner Take Nothing,* which included now-famous pieces such as "A Clean, Well-Lighted Place" and "A Way You'll Never Be." The critics took only lukewarm notice, but the book sold well, especially considering America was in the grip of a Great Depression that was hurting the sales of more jet-set fare such as his friend Fitzgerald's *The Great Gatsby.*

THE DARK CONTINENT

Ever since reading about Teddy Roosevelt's African safaris in his childhood, Hemingway had yearned to pit himself against big, dangerous animals. In the summer of 1933, he got his wish when he, Pauline, and their friend Charles Thompson traveled to the dark continent, subsidized by a twenty-five thousand dollar loan from Pauline's Uncle Gus. Their three months of exploring and hunting game proved creatively beneficial, and in 1935, a quasi-fictional version of the trip was published as *Green Hills of Africa.* Once again his work was poorly received for its self-aggrandizing digressions and pontificating. Hemingway portrayed himself, without apparent irony, as a cool-under-pressure warrior while he characterized his companions as selfish jerks. Even critic and writer Edmund Wilson, normally one of Hemingway's defenders, called it "the only book ever written which makes Africa and its animals seem dull."[12] However, the same trip yielded the inspiration for two of the most highly praised short stories Hemingway ever wrote, "The Snows of Kilimanjaro" and "The Short Happy Life of Frances Macomber." In both of these, as in much of his pure fiction, the protagonists exhibit weaknesses such as hard drinking and spinelessness that Hemingway would never have admitted to in any nonfiction or semifictional literary self-portrait. Hemingway seemed better able to distill real-life events with brute honesty when he had the window-dressing of fiction to drape over them; when writing about himself *as* himself, he was strangely image-conscious.

WAR CORRESPONDENT

In March 1937, the North American Newspaper Alliance asked Hemingway to cover the Spanish Civil War. Though Hemingway's sympathy lay with the communist loyalists who supported democratic elections, Pauline supported the regime led by Francisco Franco, which wound up winning the conflict and installing a dictatorial government in spring 1939. The Hemingway marriage was on the skids already. Ernest had met a young writer named Martha Gelhorn at Sloppy Joe's bar in Key West in December 1936, and when he returned from Spain after the war ended, one of his first acts was to divorce Pauline and move to Havana, Cuba, with Martha. They named their large house Finca Vigia ("Lookout Farm"), and Hemingway commenced work on a novel based on his most recent Spanish experiences called *For Whom the Bell Tolls*. It was published in 1940. The critical reception was Hemingway's greatest since *A Farewell to Arms*. The book was a huge best-seller. The Pulitzer Prize Committee unanimously voted it the best novel of the year, but for political reasons the result was vetoed by the president of Columbia University, and the prize went unawarded.

The 1940s were not a prolific period for Hemingway. He started at least two novels that went unpublished until after his death. The biggest distraction was World War II, which he actively participated in by operating an amateur spy ring out of Havana called the "Crook Factory," much to the displeasure of J. Edgar Hoover's FBI. Hemingway even reportedly gave chase to German submarines with his own specially outfitted ship the *Pilar*, though the full extent (and success rate) of his counterespionage capers is only now coming to light and remains hotly debated. Undebated is how annoying Martha found her husband's self-anointed war efforts, which she considered an excuse for him to fish and drink with his buddies rather than perform his writerly duty of covering the "real" war that had all Europe in flames.

Hemingway gave in to her pressure in the spring of 1944 and traveled to London, where a car crash left him with a serious concussion and a gash in his head that required fifty stitches. Martha, visiting him in the hospital, made little of his injuries, which were in fact quite serious and excruciating. Her first reaction upon seeing Hemingway's head bandaged up like he was wearing a turban was to laugh, a reaction that hurt him deeply. Baker reports that "for months thereafter he complained about his wife's 'silly inhumanity.'"[15] Hemingway had already met a petite blonde woman from northern Minnesota named Mary Welsh, who wrote for British magazines. Mary was nurturing and complimentary. Despite the fact that she was married, her affair with Ernest was long under way by the time the Allies (accompanied by Hemingway) liberated Paris in late August 1944.

THE LAST GREAT NOVEL

Hemingway did not return to America until March 1946, and curiously the only work of novel length to be produced from his entire European tour of World War II was the bittersweet *Across the River and into the Trees*, a love story about a disgraced army colonel and a young Italian countess (the colonel's shrewish ex-wife was modeled unflatteringly after Martha). Though the quality of writing was clearly up to his usual par, the book was slammed by critics as a sappy disappointment. Stung by the reception, Hemingway began writing a story about an old man's war with a giant fish that he'd been thinking about since 1936. Unlike most of his novels, this one required hardly any revisions.

The Old Man and the Sea appeared in its entirety in a single issue of *Life* magazine in September 1952 and sold more than 5 million copies. Scribner's initial hard-cover edition of fifty thousand sold out almost immediately. The novel won the Pulitzer Prize for fiction in 1953, Hemingway's first major literary prize. He was now staggeringly rich and considered the world's greatest living writer.

MEDICAL WOES

With nothing left to prove, Hemingway took it easy. He and Mary took in some Spanish bullfights, then went to Africa for a safari. There, fate dealt a bitter blow. Moments after boarding a plane for Uganda, the small craft crashed and caught fire. All but Hemingway made it out through an exit at the front of the fuselage. "Ernest appeared on the port wing, having butted his way through the jammed door with his hapless head and his damaged shoulder."[14] Afterward, the litany of his injuries read like an obituary: a fractured skull; cracked spinal discs; dislocated right arm and shoulder; a paralyzed sphincter; collapsed lower intestine; ruptured liver, kidney, and spleen; and severe burns to his arms, face, and head. Incredibly, it was the second plane crash of the trip, and though Ernest survived, the aftereffects undoubtedly contributed to what would soon become a heartbreaking downward spiral.

Refusing to be "daunted," as Harvey Stone of *The Sun Also Rises* would have said, the Hemingways continued on to Venice before returning home to Cuba. Hemingway's injuries prevented him from attending the ceremony in Sweden for his winning the Nobel Prize for literature, but his written acceptance was read to the committee by the U.S. ambassador to Sweden.

After 1954, Hemingway's decades of drinks and hurts began to catch up with him. His nearly quarter of a million words on the last safari were unpublishable in his eyes. Other unfinished projects abounded. As his body gave out, his genius too seemed to be waning, and there was nothing he could do about it.

In 1959, *Life* magazine asked him to write a piece on a series of bullfights. Hemingway spent that summer compiling what wound up ballooning into an uncharacteristically wordy product. Hemingway actually enlisted the help of his friend A.E. Hotchner in trimming it down to half its length. The article was printed in three chunky installments as "The Dangerous Summer" in 1960, the last publication Hemingway would live to see.

DEATH OF A LEGEND

Though he was only sixty, Hemingway looked twenty years older, and his drinking and despondency had become severe problems. Hemingway had begun work on his memoirs, which would be published (and praised) posthumously in 1964 as *A Moveable Feast.* In July 1960, Hemingway left Cuba for the remote environs of Ketchum, Idaho, a state he likened in its untamed primacy to Spain. But by the fall, he had been admitted to the Mayo Clinic in Rochester, Minnesota, for worsening depression that was beyond Mary's means to handle alone. His treatment included recurrent electroshock therapy, which, according to biographer Jeffrey Meyers, "instead of helping him most certainly hastened his demise."[15] A side effect of shock treatments is memory loss, which for a writer can be especially disheartening.

Now bereft of the ability to create his art, Hemingway slid deeper into depression and paranoia. Early on the morning of July 2, 1961, a little over two weeks before he would turn sixty-two, Hemingway rose, chose a shotgun from his basement closet, went upstairs, and took his own life. He left behind a legacy of printed works that to this day are numbered among the finest examples of stylistic genius any writer worldwide has ever produced.

NOTES

1. Quoted in Carlos Baker, *Ernest Hemingway.* New York: Scribner, 1969, p. 9.
2. Baker, *Ernest Hemingway,* p. 17.
3. Quoted in Baker, *Ernest Hemingway,* p. 38.
4. Quoted in Matthew J. Bruccoli, ed., *Conversations with Ernest Hemingway.* Jackson: University Press of Mississippi, 1986, p. 4.
5. Quoted in Baker, *Ernest Hemingway,* p. 100.
6. Quoted in Baker, *Ernest Hemingway,* p. 160.
7. Quoted in Baker, *Ernest Hemingway,* p. 149.
8. Quoted in Baker, *Ernest Hemingway,* p. 149.
9. Quoted in Baker, *Ernest Hemingway,* pp. 150–51.
10. Quoted in Baker, *Ernest Hemingway,* p. 170.
11. Quoted in Baker, *Ernest Hemingway,* p. 179.
12. Quoted in Baker, *Ernest Hemingway,* p. 191.
13. Quoted in Baker, *Ernest Hemingway,* p. 281.
14. Quoted in Baker, *Ernest Hemingway,* p. 391.
15. Jeffrey Meyers, ed., *Hemingway: A Biography.* New York: Da Capo Press, 1999, p. 550.

CHARACTERS AND PLOT

CHARACTERS

Jake Barnes: Jake Barnes is the novel's narrator. He is a veteran of World War I, during which he received a wound that left him impotent. He works as a journalist in Paris, where he and his friends, including Brett Ashley, engage in endless rounds of parties and drinking. His unrequited love for Brett, who was his nurse in the hospital where he recovered, causes them both great anguish. As hard a drinker as any of his circle, he still seems the most stable personality among them. He is an observer who reveals little about himself directly while acting as Brett's crutch and trying to keep peace between the rest of his friends.

Brett Ashley: Brett Ashley is a promiscuous British socialite. Her first love died of dysentery during World War I. She worked in the hospital where Jake recovered from his wound. She may or may not have loved Jake then but sees his wound as a barrier to any sexual relationship. Her first husband, Lord Ashley, was also a war veteran but was psychologically traumatized by the war and often threatened to kill her, sleeping with a loaded service revolver. Brett is awaiting a divorce from him when the novel opens. She is currently engaged to Mike Campbell, a bankrupt alcoholic Scotsman, but is also involved in brief flings with Robert Cohn and Pedro Romero.

Mike Campbell: Mike Campbell is an abrasive, alcoholic, bankrupt war veteran from Scotland and is engaged to Brett Ashley. He has a seething temper that combusts the more he drinks. He has great trouble coping with Brett's promiscuity but singles out Robert Cohn in particular as a target for his hostility.

Robert Cohn: Robert Cohn, born to a prosperous Jewish family in New York, threw himself into boxing at Princeton to counter anti-Semitism and there became middleweight champion. He married soon after graduation and had three children, but after five years and the diminishment of his fifty-thousand-dollar inheritance, his wife left him, much to his relief. While editing a literary magazine, he met Frances Coyne, with whom he moved to Paris. He becomes infatuated with Brett Ashley at first sight, and after a brief tryst with her, he refuses to believe his deep passion is not reciprocated. Unlike the rest of the circle of friends, Cohn is a light drinker and believes in the prewar ideals of romance, which annoys his more jaded companions. As a Jewish nonveteran, he is the group's premiere and constant whipping boy.

Frances Coyne: Frances Coyne is a manipulative, image-conscious status seeker who latches on to Cohn in the hopes of rising socially through him but becomes possessive and jealous when he transfers his affections to Brett Ashley. With the fading of her looks, she has become intent on getting Cohn to marry her, but the success of his novel and then his introduction to Brett Ashley trample those dreams. Livid and bitter when he breaks off their engagement, she still accepts his two-hundred-pound buyout and leaves for England so that he can pursue Brett.

Bill Gorton: Bill Gorton, another alcoholic war veteran, lives and works in New York City but travels to Europe for his summer vacation and joins Jake for a fishing trip in Burguete, Spain, followed by the annual fiesta in Pamplona. He is attracted to Brett until he finds out how far back his place in line is. Like Jake, he enjoys Cohn's friendship at first but later joins in referring to him contemptuously.

Count Mippipopolous: Count Mippipopolous is a veteran of seven wars. He also is attracted to Brett but, unlike the rest, does not act proprietary with her. Compared with the novel's other characters, the count is the authoritative voice of reason. He believes in love but not in Cohn's idealized way. He stands apart from the shallow age in which he now finds himself, living by a system of pleasure principles to which he assigns absolute values.

Montoya: Montoya runs an inn in Pamplona that he keeps ready for Jake year after year. He and Jake share an aficionado's love of bullfighting, and he sets Jake apart from the shallow swarms of tourists who converge on Pamplona every year for the fiesta. He considers Jake's friends, especially Brett, corrupting influences, and he writes Jake off forever when Jake facilitates Brett's liaison with Pedro Romero.

Pedro Romero: Pedro Romero is a gorgeous nineteen-year-old bullfighter who symbolizes all that is noble in the sport. Unlike his colleagues, he does not ratchet up false impressions of danger but works closely and gracefully with the bulls in a way aficionados like Jake and Montoya can appreciate. When Brett has an affair with him, he asks her to marry him, but she eventually terminates the relationship because she fears ruining him and his career.

PLOT SUMMARY

Book I (Chapters 1–7)

Jake Barnes, Frances Coyne, and Robert Cohn are eating out together. Jake suggests he and Cohn go to Strasbourg because he knows a girl there who can show them around. Frances kicks him under the table a few times before Jake lets up. Afterward, Cohn follows Jake to reprimand him for suggesting such an endeavor in front of her.

Cohn acquires new cockiness when his book goes over well with the critics. Though women have been throwing themselves at him, he feels unfulfilled. His next step in life, he has decided, is to travel to South America. He unsuccessfully tries to coax Jake into going with him, offering to pay all expenses. Jake tells him only bullfighters live their lives "all the way up" and that "you can't get away from yourself by moving from one place to another."

Later that evening, sitting alone in a café, Jake has a bout of loneliness and catches the eye of an indigenous prostitute, Georgette. They go to a restaurant by horse cab, and along the way Jake rebuffs the pass she makes at him, explaining that he received a wound in the war which limits his sexual ability. They concur that the war "perhaps would have been better avoided." They are spotted by Jake's friends and invited to a dance club, where they encounter Brett Ashley. Cohn is instantly smitten but his advances seem to have little effect, and she leaves the club in Jake's company.

In the taxi, Brett declares that she is miserable but rebuffs Jake's kisses. She returns his love to some extent but is unwilling to consider a relationship with him because of his wound. They go to a café and drink some more. There someone introduces them to Count Mippipopolous.

Jake goes home and wishes he had never met Brett. He starts to cry but drifts off to sleep. After four in the morning, Brett bursts drunkenly into his apartment, reporting that the count is waiting outside in his car and has offered her ten thousand dollars to go to Biarritz with him, an offer she refused. She wants Jake to go out with them. He tries to get her to stay, kissing her, but finally they make an appointment to meet.

Cohn meets Jake at his office the next day for lunch and asks about Brett. Jake's unflattering responses and news that she is slated to marry Scotsman Mike Campbell get a rise out of Cohn, but Jake pacifies him and changes the subject. That night, Brett misses their appointment.

Cohn finds Jake later and they unwind in a café, where Frances appears and asks to speak to Jake alone. She tells Jake that Cohn has broken off their engagement, and she fears no man will ever want her now. They then return to Cohn, where Frances bitterly announces that she has wrangled two hundred pounds out of Cohn so that she can return to England, where she anticipates visits with "friends" who will not want her around. Cohn sits silent through the blistering barrage. Jake excuses himself.

The count and Brett visit Jake at his place. She claims she missed their "date" because she was drunk, but Jake does not believe her. Brett sends the count to fetch champagne, and Jake asks why they cannot live together. She says her constant affairs will make him unhappy and that she plans to leave for San Sebastian because it will be better for both of them.

The count, a veteran of seven wars and four revolutions, explains that he tries to enjoy everything in life. The secret is "to get to know the values." He is always in love because that is a value he cherishes. The count asks why Brett and Jake do not get married and they give evasive responses. Brett's mood deteriorates, and Jake accompanies her to her hotel. She refuses to let him come up, and after a few awkward kisses pushes him away and dramatically sighs that she will never see him again.

Book II (Chapters 8–18)
Jake gets a note from Cohn saying he has gone to the country. Frances has set sail for England. Bill Gorton, Jake's friend from the United States, arrives to attend the Pamplona fiesta. They have dinner with Brett and Mike, who express an interest in going to Spain as well. When they are alone, Brett asks Jake if he thinks it will be too "rough" for Cohn if he attends as well. She then reveals she had a quick affair with Cohn in

San Sebastian. Jake, though not thrilled by this disclosure, arranges to meet her and Mike in Spain as requested.

Cohn meets Jake and Bill in Bayonne, where they hire a car to Pamplona. Cohn is edgy because he is not sure the others know of his tryst with Brett and openly doubts that she and Mike will appear on schedule. Bill, irritated by Cohn's "superior and Jewish" airs, wagers a hundred pesetas they will. When returning with the bullfight tickets, Jake stops by a church to pray but is unable to concentrate. Cohn, in his Sunday best, goes to meet Brett and Mike at the station, Jake in attendance to deliberately irritate him. Mike and Brett are a no-show but send along a telegram explaining that they have stopped off in San Sebastian.

The next day, Cohn, whom Jake now actively detests, announces he is staying behind to wait for Brett and Mike, whom he believes meant to meet him in San Sebastian, while Jake and Bill take a bus to Burguete to go fishing. When Bill has Jake alone, Bill tells him that Cohn had confided in him about his rendezvous with Brett. Bill thinks Cohn is nice but "so awful."

Bill and Jake get drunk on the contents of a wineskin passed around by the Basque passengers on the bus. When they arrive, the innkeeper charges them a high price for their room because it is "the big season," though they are the only ones staying there. When they learn the wine is included, they drink several bottles.

The next day they catch ten large trout. They banter, drink two more bottles of wine, eat lunch, and nap. Bill asks Jake how he feels about Brett, and Jake admits he has loved her off and on for many years and would appreciate a change of subject. They spend five days there in the company of an Englishman they hit it off with named Harris. Jake gets a letter from Mike explaining that Brett passed out on the train and they are running a few days late.

When Bill and Jake arrive in Pamplona, the innkeeper, Montoya, has Jake's "usual" room ready. He sees Jake as a fellow aficionado of the bullfights, not a poseur like the other tourists. Bill and Jake find Brett, Mike, and Cohn in a café, then go to watch the unloading of the bulls. When these engines of destruction charge from their cages, steers are used to calm them, and often get gored in the process. Jake tells Brett not to look at the bloodshed, but she is enraptured. Jake explains, without apparent irony, that bulls are dangerous when they are alone, separated from the herd.

Afterward, they go to a café and get drunk. Mike cuts Cohn down for following Brett around "like a steer" and for not knowing when he is not wanted. Bill intercedes, leading Cohn away. Mike shouts that Brett has had affairs before but never "with Jews." More food and liberal amounts of wine are consumed.

Exploding rockets herald the start of the fiesta at noon on July 6. Seven days of nonstop drinking, dancing, and music ensue. The crowd pulls Jake and his friends into a dancing circle around Brett, whom the celebrants treat as divine. The next morning Jake watches the crowd run ahead of the bulls through the streets toward the bullring. Montoya introduces Jake to a promising new matador, Pedro Romero, who is nineteen years old and the "best-looking boy" Jake has ever seen. Brett is quite taken with Pedro and his green pants and marvels at his skill. She has watched everything, including the ritual goring of the horses, while Cohn has been unable to take the sight without getting queasy, for which Mike rides him mercilessly. Brett and Mike watch the next bullfight with Jake. Romero works close to the bull with great artistry, wearing it down slowly before making the kill.

The American ambassador to Spain asks Montoya to give Pedro a message inviting him to dine at the Grand Hotel. Montoya consults Jake about this offer, and Jake agrees with him that Pedro's association with "foreigners" would be a corrupting influence and advises him not to deliver the message. Jake has dinner with his friends and there encounters Pedro, who is modest but passionate about his work. Brett convinces Jake to introduce them to Pedro. Pedro drinks cognac and warms to Brett, which Montoya watches with disapproval. Montoya never again acknowledges Jake's presence. After Pedro leaves, Mike lays into Cohn again, and Jake drags him away to avert a fight.

The next day, Brett savagely orders Cohn to leave her alone so she can dine alone with Jake. Brett asks Jake if he still loves her. When he says "yes," she begs him to set her up with Pedro, with whom she has become blindly infatuated. Jake complies and later finds they have gone off to her room together.

Jake meets Mike and Bill in a café. Soon Cohn shows up, demanding that Jake tell him where Brett is. Mike tells him she has "gone off with the bullfighter chap," and Cohn calls

Jake a pimp. All three get into a fistfight; Cohn is the last one standing. When Jake drags himself back to the hotel, a tearful Cohn begs him to shake hands and forgive him. Jake finally shakes hands but forgives nothing.

The next morning, a man is killed during the release of the bulls. Jake learns that Cohn found Brett and Pedro, and the two men fought. After Brett's tongue-lashing, Cohn begged Pedro to shake hands, but Pedro slugged him in response. Cohn leaves Pamplona. Brett meets the rest of the group at a café the next day and reports that Pedro looks battered but plans to bullfight anyway. Mike mutters, "Brett's got a bullfighter. She had a Jew named Cohn, but he turned out badly." Brett whisks Jake away as Mike overturns the table. Brett wants Jake to take her to a church so she can pray for Pedro but gets the shakes once there, and so they return to the café.

At the last bullfight, Pedro faces the bull that killed the man earlier and kills it with elegance, to the crowd's delight. Its notched ear is cut off and given to Brett, who absently leaves it behind in her hotel room drawer when she leaves that night.

Book III (Chapter 19)

Mike, Bill, and Jake share a car to Bayonne, get drunk, and drop Mike off. Jake leaves Bill and takes the morning train to San Sebastian, where he spends time swimming. The act restores him just in time to receive a pair of fresh telegrams from Brett, one forwarded from Paris, the other from Pamplona. She is "in trouble" and needs him to come to the Hotel Montana in Madrid.

Brett greets Jake with a kiss. She explains that although Pedro wanted to marry her, she sent him away because she did not want to ruin him. She intends to go back to Mike. She and Jake go to a bar and have a few martinis, then dinner with several bottles of wine. They get a taxi and drive around. Jake puts his arm around her and Brett says, "Oh, Jake, we could have had such a damned good time together." To which he replies, "Yes, isn't it pretty to think so?"

CHAPTER 1

Settings in *The Sun Also Rises*

READINGS ON
THE SUN ALSO RISES

The Differences Between France and Spain

Delbert E. Wylder

Delbert E. Wylder is the author of many works on a variety of writers, including Hemingway, William Eastlake, and Edward Abbey. In this excerpt from his book *Hemingway's Heroes*, Wylder claims that Hemingway contrasts two very different European cultures through which Jake Barnes struggles to find solace: France as materialistic and Spain as spiritual. Both have their place in Jake's life, and both are necessary for the maintenance of his mental health.

Part of the awareness the reader has of Jake's sensitivity results from [an] important aspect of his character, an extremely important one in terms of his role as narrator: Jake is almost completely honest. It is partly this honesty of Jake's, his ability to discuss the reasons for his actions that makes the reader accept his narrative. But unfortunately the reader then sometimes fails to find beneath the surface of the story as Jake tells it a double dichotomy that is part of the very structure of the novel. There is a physical or geographical emphasis which allows a contrast between the countries of France and Spain and there is a psychological emphasis which stresses significant contrasts between the characters.

FRANCE VS. SPAIN

The geographical dichotomy is made especially clear in Book III, which functions essentially as an epilogue. Book I (roughly sixty-seven pages) had been set in France; Book II (roughly 155 pages), primarily in Spain; and the action of Book III (twenty pages) shifts between the two countries. In the epilogue Jake reflects on his experiences in a rather conscious summing up and emphasizes the contrast between

Excerpted from *Hemingway's Heroes,* by Delbert E. Wylder. Copyright © 1969 The University of New Mexico Press. Reprinted by permission of The University of New Mexico Press.

the two nations; they then become symbolic of two attitudes toward life: one essentially materialistic and sterile, the other more primitive and more virile—in a sense, almost romantic. Neither country provides an easy answer to the problem of living one's life, as Jake Barnes discovers. Life in Spain, however, finally has a more lasting effect on him.

The materialistic world of France is the easier to live in. As Jake comments,

> The waiter seemed a little offended about the flowers of the Pyrenees, so I overtipped him. That made him happy. It felt comfortable to be in a country where it is so simple to make people happy. You can never tell whether a Spanish waiter will thank you. Everything is on such a clear financial basis in France. It is the simplest country to live in. No one makes things complicated by becoming your friend for any obscure reason. If you want people to like you, you have only to spend a little money. I spent a little money and the waiter liked me. He appreciated my valuable qualities. He would be glad to see me back. I would dine there again some time and he would be glad to see me, and would want me at his table. It would be a sincere liking because it would have a sound basis. I was back in France.

Within the passage is a direct contrast between the waiters of France and Spain and an implied contrast between the two countries. The French waiter operates materialistically, objectively, and predictably. The Spanish waiter, it is suggested, is motivated by "obscure" reasons that make human relationships extremely difficult. Life is less complicated in France because the value systems are materialistically defined. There are no problems of abstract values and emotional responses that confuse relationships. There is irony, of course, in Jake's remark, for the important point has been developed throughout the novel that France is sterile, and this statement of contrast in the epilogue makes clear a dichotomy that has existed beneath the surface of the novel.

Jake's value system is very much like that of Count Mippipopolous, the high priest of materialism in the novel. Count Mippipopolous has a rigid system of values, and he states that the "secret" is getting to know the values. Wine and women have a strong place in his values, and he pays for his enjoyment. Love does not complicate his life because he is always in love without being emotionally involved. But Brett sagely identifies his state of being. "You haven't any values," she says. "You're dead, that's all." Brett is right. Unlike the bullfighters, who live their lives "all the way up,"

Count Mippipopolous has quit living. It is ironically symbolic that Book I ends with a highly emotional scene between Brett and Jake, and that before going up to bed, Jake is driven home by the Count's chauffeur. Jake has just unhappily said goodbye to Brett. He has lost in his emotional life, but he receives deference from the chauffeur because he tips him. "I gave him twenty francs and he touched his cap and said: 'Good night, sir,' and drove off."

The sterility of France and of both Jake's and the Count's value systems is made quite clear in a scene between Jake and Bill Gorton just after the latter has arrived in Paris.

"Here's a taxidermist's," Bill said. "Want to buy anything? Nice stuffed dog?"

"Come on," I said. "You're pie-eyed."

"Pretty nice stuffed dogs," Bill said. "Certainly brighten up your flat."

"Come on."

"Just one stuffed dog. I can take 'em or leave 'em alone. But listen, Jake. Just one stuffed dog."

"Come on."

"Mean everything in the world to you after you bought it. Simple exchange of values. You give them money. They give you a stuffed dog."

One pays money for a stuffed rather than live animal. It is a simple, but meaningless, exchange of values. One notes, too, that France is the country of statues, men in stone, and most of them in some act of waving flags or raising swords. In contrast, Spain is the country of live animals—of bulls, of horses, of fish in the streams. And the men who posture with baton or sword are alive—Romero or Belmonte profiling to kill, or the policeman raising his baton in the last paragraph of the novel. This difference between countries is made even more explicit in the characterization and the description of customs.

Jake's concierge in Paris is an example of the materialistic Parisian.

Her life-work lay in the pelouse, but she kept an eye on the people of the pesage, and she took great pride in telling me which of my guests were well brought up, which were of good family, who were sportsmen, a French word pronounced with the accent on the men. The only trouble was that people who did not fall into any of these three categories were very liable to be told there was no one home, chez Barnes.

It is this concierge, as a matter of fact, who, very much like the French waiter already discussed, judges Brett Ashley by the type of tip she leaves. Lady Brett alienates the concierge on her first visit to Jake's apartment, but the latter is reconciled when Brett gives her far too much of the Count's money. After the tip, the concierge says, "It was the one who was here last night. In the end I find she is very nice."

In Spain, during the bus trip to the fishing location, Bill and Jake stop for a rest at a *posada*. They go inside for a drink, and then encounter the contrasting rural Spanish attitude toward tipping. "We each had an aguardiente and paid forty centimes for the two drinks. I gave the woman fifty centimes to make a tip, and she gave me back the copper piece, thinking I had misunderstood the price."

Almost all of the people in France operate on the cash-value materialistic principle. This is seen especially in those people who have anything to do with the American tourists. As Jake reports,

> We ate dinner at Madame Lecomte's restaurant on the far side of the island. It was crowded with Americans and we had

SPAIN: THE LAST GOOD COUNTRY

Just like Jake Barnes, Hemingway was drawn to a fiesta concept of life and considered Spain a healing place, especially unspoiled hideaways such as Burguete.

In [Hemingway's] forty years of contacts with Spain, there was a symbiosis unique in the history of literature. Other foreigners have known as much or more about the Iberian Peninsula, but none has made such an imaginative rendering of the country and its people in his work. Ernesto, as his Spanish friends called him—out of both affection and an inability to pronounce his surname—said that Spain was the country he loved more than any other except his own. Dozens of newspaper and magazine articles, some of his best short stories, four of his books, the one play, and the only movie in which he participated directly all deal with the peninsula. He spent a total of some three years on Spanish soil. He knew the people of all classes and regions, their artists and writers of the past and present. He knew the landscape the way he had known the plains of Illinois before they were built over, the hunting and fishing grounds of the West, the coast of south Florida. He

to stand up and wait for a place. Some one had put it in the American Women's Club list as a quaint restaurant on the Paris quais as yet untouched by Americans, so we had to wait forty-five minutes for a table. Bill had eaten at the restaurant in 1918, and right after the armistice, and Madame Lecomte made a great fuss over seeing him.

"Doesn't get us a table, though," Bill said. "Grand woman, though."

This kind of treatment, as contrasted to that given Jake and Bill by the hotel-keeper Montoya in Spain, emphasizes the basic satiric contrast between the two countries. Bill's recognition that the earlier friendship with Madame Lecomte has not helped at all in getting them fed is contrasted to Montoya's carefully reserving Jake's usual rooms.

From the very beginning of their journey into Spain, Jake and Bill encounter friendly people. They, as American tourists, are treated with friendliness and hospitality by the peasants on the bus. The peasants insist that the two drink from the Spanish winebags. Even commercial people are friendly. During the fiesta Jake leaves a bar to buy some wineskins. When the salesman discovers that Jake wants to

---

knew Spain's language, smells, sounds, wines, foods, roads, birds, animals, trees, skies, and how the weather was. "I love Spain the way I love Idaho, Wyoming and Montana," he said, "and I feel just as much at home. In Madrid I feel more at home than in New York."

Almost everything about Hemingway bore a trace of Spain, from his art to the houses he chose to live in. His build and size, for example, were unmistakably American, but Spaniards who knew him have told me that his bearing, gestures, élan, and penchant for obscenity made him resemble their countrymen. Like the partly autobiographical Frederic Henry in *A Farewell to Arms,* Hemingway probably passed more than once for a "Latin." In his physical presence there was a kind of vital intensity, perhaps born from danger and exposure to death, that recalled the matador's. The dark or night side of his personality (what he called "black ass") found its closest parallel in the Spanish sense of nada—the anguish of nightmare, oblivion, and death—a realm of terror and the grotesque evoked by some of his favorite Spanish artists like Goya, Quevedo, and Picasso.

Edward F. Stanton, *Hemingway and Spain: A Pursuit,* pp. xiv–xv.

use them for the purpose for which they were made, and not to sell in France, he is very considerate.

"What are you going to do? Sell them in Bayonne?"

"No. Drink out of them."

He slapped me on the back.

"Good man. Eight pesetas for the two. The lowest price."

The man who was stencilling the new ones and tossing them into a pile stopped.

"It's true," he said. "Eight pesetas is cheap."

Spain is a country where materialism has not yet penetrated—at least not in certain areas. Where it has been introduced, symbolized by modern plumbing, things are beginning to change. But even in these places, the Spaniards feel guilty about their materialism.

I went out to find the woman and ask her how much the room and board was. She put her hands under her apron and looked away from me.

"Twelve pesetas."

"Why, we only paid that in Pamplona."

She did not say anything, just took off her glasses and wiped them on her apron.

"That's too much," I said. "We didn't pay more than that at a big hotel."

"We've put in a bathroom.". . .

"LIVE" AND "DEAD" SPORTS

The contrast between France and Spain is most highly developed in the disparity between the national "sports" of the two countries. The emphasis that Hemingway places on bullfighting is easily recognized through Jake Barnes' interest in it and his feeling for it. We see something of the traditional and ritualistic aspects of the bullfight in Jake's description. We also note his admiration for the meaningfulness of the forms of the bullfight and of the passes, and the recognition that each *torero* tests his integrity each time he encounters the bull. Furthermore, the *torero* faces death, not as the man who is killed during the unloading and running of the bulls, but in an art form where each act has not only beauty but meaning. The whole ceremony, then, is the antithesis of the meaningless world Jake Barnes and his friends live in. This is the "sport" of Spain. Jake Barnes is one of the initiated who have *afición*, who have the subjective feeling about what goes on in the bullring, and who understand the deeper meanings behind the bullfight. He does not react emotionally only, like those who fail to give Juan Belmonte his due, but can appreciate artistically both the worth of the young Romero and the great dignity of Belmonte in this "sport" which is played always in the face of death.

Bicycle racing, the contrasting sport of France, is another thing. Having lunch with the team manager of one of the bicycle manufacturers, Jake is told that the Tour de France is "the greatest sporting event in the world." But there is no dignity in bicycle racing. It is, if it can be called such, a materialistic sport, where everything important can be taken care of, and where there is very little of the element of chance. As Jake reports, "[The bicycle riders] did not take the race seriously except among themselves. They had raced among themselves so often that it did not make much difference who won. Especially in a foreign country. The money could be arranged."

There is neither the dignity nor the heavy masculinity of the bullfighter in the picture of the bicycle racers. The racers have a following of French girls with "Rue de Faubourg Montmartre chic" who seem to be almost community property, for Jake cannot make out which girl belongs to which racer. The racers whisper jokes they think the girls should not hear, and then will not repeat them. They are quite unlike Romero, who remains with his cuadrilla apart from society until the point when he quite aggressively approaches Brett. He is so direct that Jake can analyze his every move and correctly interprets his glance that indicates things are "understood." Nor are the bicycle racers exposed, as Romero is, to a horn wound or fatality. Bicycle racing does not involve the potentially tragic element of a direct confrontation with death. The leader of the bicycle racers ridiculously has an attack of boils which forces him to sit on the small of his back. He blushes when one of the girls hears him tell how he is going to ride the next day with the air touching his boils. These are sportsmen, not men. Jake makes no direct comparison of bicycle racing to the bullfight, but he does make one ironic comment that makes the point beautifully. "The Spaniards, they [the French] said, did not know how to pedal." The mechanical act of pedalling is completely unimportant in contrast to the traditions and meaningful forms of the bullfight. Jake, who travels annually from one country to another as though on a religious pilgrimage, and who watches almost all of the preliminary activities as well as the bullfight itself, does not bother to watch the bicycle racers start the next morning. In fact, he indicates to the team manager that he would prefer not to be wakened for the event. . . .

Spain, then, is at the center of tradition and represents the old truths, the old concepts, the old ways. France is the new way, the materialistic direction, the country of twentieth-century change. The movement between two countries is especially important in terms of a parallel development in the cast of characters. The novel begins in France, where there are no meaningful rituals and, of course, no heroes. Jake's coterie of friends intrude upon his planned vacation with Bill Gorton and enter into the land of meaning. After Jake and Bill return from their fishing trip in the mountains the stage is set for the representatives of the materialistic world to make their impact on the world of tradition. Although Jake at first chooses to remain loyal to his Paris friends, the final victory is won by Romero, the representative of Spain. He wins because this is the land of tradition, a land where the hero may still live. And the victory of the hero has a strong effect on Jake Barnes. The geographical movement in the novel parallels and enforces the gradual shift in emphasis from one character to another.

Jake "Wins" in Spain at the End of *The Sun Also Rises*

Donald A. Daiker

Donald A. Daiker is a professor of English at Miami University and editor of many manuals, including *Composition in the Twentieth Century: Crisis and Change*. In the following viewpoint, Daiker argues that Madrid is the site of Jake Barnes's final triumph over Brett Ashley in Book III. As with much else in the novel, Daiker claims a little digging is necessary to grasp Hemingway's intentions but Jake emerges from the book as a much more successful man than he was at the outset.

Until a decade ago *The Sun Also Rises* had usually been interpreted as a chronicle of a lost generation, as an expression of nihilism, or as a representation, in Philip Young's words, of "motion which goes no place." [Beginning in the 1960s,] however, some critics—though still in the minority—have discerned in Hemingway's novel a pattern of development; they have argued that at the end of the story Jake Barnes and Brett Ashley are not back where they started, that Jake has gained in self-mastery and acquired at least a measure of control in his relationship with Brett. Surprisingly, even those who assert that Jake is a developing character pay scant attention to the crucial Book III. Although Hemingway underscores its importance through its positioning and its brevity (it consists of but one chapter), Book III has usually been dismissed with brief mention of Jake's symbolic cleansing at San Sebastian and of his ironic statement which concludes the novel. A close reading of Book III reveals, I believe, that *The Sun Also Rises* is basically an affirmative book. Hemingway's first serious novel affirms through the characterization of Jake Barnes that man can get his money's worth

Excerpted from "The Affirmative Conclusion of *The Sun Also Rises*," by Donald A. Daiker, *McNeese Review*, vol. 21 (1974–1975). Reprinted with permission.

in life, that he can learn how to live in the world. By the end of the story, Jake's sun has risen, and there is no suggestion that it will set.

THE CLEANSING AFTERMATH

Book III opens with images of washing and cleansing. The fiesta finally over, waiters "were sweeping the streets and sprinkling them with a hose." One waiter, carrying a "bucket of water and a cloth," began "to tear down the notices, pulling the paper off in strips and washing and rubbing away the paper that stuck to the stone." Since in Pamplona Jake has defiled himself, betrayed Montoya, and profaned his *afficion* by acceding to Brett's request to help her sleep with Romero, his description reflects his own need for emotional cleansing and spiritual purification. Jake recognizes the truth of Cohn's calling him a "pimp," making him feel worse at the end of Book II than at any other point in the novel. "I feel like hell," he tells Bill Gorton, and he later adds, "I was drunker than I ever remembered having been." Because Jake, like Hemingway, defines immorality as "things that made you disgusted afterward," Jake's pimping ranks as his most immoral act. The closing of Book II—"The three of us sat at the table, and it seemed as though about six people were missing"—indicates Jake's sense of loss and, in echoing a casualty report, reinforces earlier suggestions that the fiesta has been another war for Jake, wounding him emotionally as World War I had injured him physically. Yet even at the nadir of self-revulsion, there are signs of new awareness growing within Jake. In telling Mike Campbell "I'm blind," he not only acknowledges that he is drunk but more importantly hints that he is beginning to realize the cost to himself and others of his failure to see clearly the nature of his relationship to Brett. When Jake says, "I looked strange to myself in the glass," he vaguely recognizes himself for what he has been: a panderer at least partially responsible for Cohn's bloody beating of Romero, for Mike's increased drunkenness, and for his own self-contempt. It is precisely this "strange" self which Jake seeks to wipe out and which creates his need for washing and cleansing, for the waters, of San Sebastian. . . .

SAN SEBASTIAN

At San Sebastian the activity described in greatest detail is Jake's swimming. It relates to Romero's bullfighting in that each is a ritual act which functions in part to cleanse and purify. His face and body smashed by Cohn's fists, Romero in the bull ring "was wiping all that out now. Each thing that he did with this bull wiped that out a little cleaner." Although Jake, too, wipes out the degrading experiences of Pamplona in the waters of San Sebastian, his task is quite different from Romero's. "The fight with Cohn had not touched his [Romero's] spirit," but Jake has suffered both physical and spiritual defeat. He has been physically beaten by Cohn and spiritually defeated by his inability to resist Brett's appeal for help. Foolishly clinging to the unrealistic notion that he and Brett can somehow develop a meaningful and permanent relationship, Jake moves closer to the position of the romantic Robert Cohn, as suggested by his sleeping in Cohn's room and wearing Cohn's jacket. Just as Cohn is prepared "to do battle for his lady love," Jake asks Brett, "What do you want me to do?" and "Anything you want me to do?" Aware of his vulnerability, Jake had accurately foreseen that given "the proper chance" he would "be as big an ass as Cohn." If Cohn is an emotional adolescent throughout the novel—even during his last appearance he sports his Princeton polo shirt—Jake also acts immaturely at Pamplona. His telling Cohn "Don't call me Jake" and his making Cohn take back the name "pimp" represent the same kind of prep-school stuff for which he had earlier chided Cohn. In agreeing to shake hands with Cohn, as Romero would not, Jake tacitly acknowledges that he and Cohn are linked by their falsely romantic attitude toward Brett and by their lack of self-control.

Thus when Jake goes to San Sebastian, he attempts not only to wipe out his degrading experiences in Pamplona but also to re-create his inner self. Because Jake expects eventually to be summoned by Brett, he consciously strives to build a stronger self, one capable of recognizing the self-destructive nature of his relationship to Brett, subduing his passion for her, and resisting her appeals whenever they threaten his manhood. Jake's swimming and diving symbolically represent his efforts toward self-renewal. During the first day at San Sebastian Jake swims out to the raft and tries several dives:

> I dove deep once, swimming down to the bottom. I swam with my eyes open and it was green and dark. The raft made a dark shadow. I came out of water beside the raft, pulled up, dove once more, holding it for length, and then swam ashore.

In swimming to the bottom of the sea, Jake is figuratively probing the depths of his inner self. There he clearly recognizes the darkness and confusion which has motivated his conduct. Although the "dark shadow" of Jake's past hovers over him, he will build upon it, use it as a learning experience, pull himself up by it to create a new self. In this sense Jake's diving deep suggests that his new self will have depth and a sound basis; his holding the second dive "for length" signifies that his new self will last and survive.

When on the next morning Jake sees "Nurses in uniform" and a wounded soldier, forcefully reminding him of the conditions under which he met Brett, he is not emotionally upset. Yet just as Brett in the past has made it difficult for Jake to preserve his emotional equilibrium, so this recollection makes it more difficult for him to stay afloat while swimming. He encounters rough surf and rollers, which force him "to dive sometimes." Although such swimming tires Jake, the water feels "buoyant and cold," making him feel "as though you could never sink." Having gained in self-confidence, Jake thinks he "would like to swim across the bay" but is "afraid of cramp." The swim across the bay represents for Jake the ultimate test; symbolically, it anticipates his next direct encounter with Brett which will take place in Madrid. Although Jake's fear of cramp indicates that the outcome of that encounter, as of a bullfight, is in doubt, his final dive and swim suggest a newly won sense of power, purpose, and self-control:

> After a while I stood up, gripped with my toes on the edge of the raft as it tipped with my weight, and dove cleanly and deeply, to come up through the lightening water, blew the salt water out of my head, and swam slowly and steadily in to shore.

JAKE PAYS HIS TAB

When Jake returns to his hotel he is handed a telegram that had been forwarded from Paris: "COULD YOU COME HOTEL MONTANA MADRID AM RATHER IN TROUBLE BRETT." Moments later a postman with a "big moustache" looking "very military" delivers an identically worded telegram that had been forwarded from Pamplona. The military appearance of the postman who brings Brett's telegram suggests a link between Brett and the war. Each is able to wound Jake: the war injures Jake physically; Brett damages Jake emotionally. Moreover, each produces within Jake a loss of self-control, a "feeling of things coming that you could not prevent happening." Jake's receiving two telegrams from Brett forcefully drives home the repetitive quality of their relationship. In Book I Brett had told Jake, "I've been so miserable," implicitly asking him to relieve her misery. In Book II she begged Jake to "stay by me and see me through this." In Book III, again "rather in trouble," Brett again solicits Jake's help. Although Jake had earlier sensed the circular, unprogressive nature of their relationship—"I had the feeling . . . of it all being something repeated, something I had been through and that now I *must* go through again" (italics mine)—he had felt impotent to change it. Now he feels differently, and his refusal to tip the concierge for the second telegram as he had for the first indicates his determination to break the pattern of repetition.

If Jake is angered by Brett's telegram—"that meant San Sebastian all shot to hell"—he nevertheless feels responsible for Brett because of his part in arranging her affair with Romero. Thus he wires Brett that he is coming, but his thoughts indicate that it will be a changed Jake who arrives in Madrid:

> That seemed to handle it. That was it. Send a girl off with one man. Introduce her to another to go off with him. Now go and bring her back. And sign the wire with love. That was it all right.

For the first time in the novel Jake looks with brutal honesty at his relationship with Brett. Frankly admitting to himself that he has been the panderer in Brett's liaison with Romero, he also acknowledges that he has been in part the cause of Brett's going off with Cohn. He realizes that, in Cohn's case, the sense of frustration created within Brett by being with the man she loves but with whom she cannot live causes her to escape an impossible situation by running off with any convenient male. Jake realizes, then, that his relationship with Brett is mutually destructive. Its continuance encourages Brett's promiscuity by allowing her to rationalize her actions even as it condemns Jake to nights spent crying in his room and days filled with feelings of self-revulsion. In repeating "that was it," Jake not only makes clear that he recognizes the irony of a "love" which destroys its participants but also seems to suggest that "this is it," that this is the end.

Jake travels to Madrid to see Brett, then, for three reasons. First, he knows that "the bill always came," that his having to extricate Brett from trouble in Madrid is one way in which he must pay for the pimping that caused it. Second, he realizes that physical escape from Brett provides no solution to his problem; he had earlier told Cohn that "going to another country doesn't make any difference. I've tried all that. You can't get away from yourself by moving from one place to another." Third, he follows Romero's example in subjecting himself to "the maximum of exposure." Jake is fully exposed, of course, only when with Brett.

JAKE THE PERPETUAL MATADOR

The image of the bullfight provides the framework for understanding the final encounter between Jake and Brett. The meeting with Brett gives "the sensation of coming tragedy," for Jake risks his emotional life in Madrid as surely as the bullfighter risks his physical life in the bull ring. When Jake reveals that on the train to Madrid he "did not sleep much," recalling his sleepless nights in Paris, his vulnerability is underscored. Arriving in Madrid Jake says: "The Norte station in Madrid is the end of the line. All trains finish there. They don't go on anywhere." Their symbolic significance established through repetition, these sentences hint that Madrid will be the end of the line for Jake. Whether Jake has merely reached "dead end,". . . or whether he will effectively end his destructive relationship with Brett remains at this point problematic, further building the tension necessary to produce "tragic sensations." In its extreme heat Madrid resembles Paris and Pamplona, testing places where Jake has suffered emotional defeat because he has allowed Brett to dominate him. Moreover, the Hotel Montana where Brett is staying sounds remarkably like Pamplona's Hotel Montoya, the scene of Jake's most recent failure. All the elements necessary to create the impression of imminent tragedy are present.

But Hemingway subtly yet decisively shows through his masterful selection of details that Jake wins a final victory over Brett and over his old, ineffectual, romantic self. The principal technique Hemingway uses is juxtaposition: he carefully contrasts the present and past relationship of Jake and Brett in order to suggest that their roles are reversed, that Jake rather than Brett is fully in control of the situation. For example, in Paris Brett had come to Jake's apartment whereas in Madrid Jake comes to Brett's room. Brett had earlier experienced difficulty getting by Jake's concierge, but now Jake finds that the hotel operator is reluctant to admit him to Brett's room. Whereas Brett had found Jake in bed when she visited his Paris apartment, now Jake finds Brett in bed. In Paris it was Jake who kissed Brett when they were alone together for the first time; in Madrid it is Brett who kisses Jake. Earlier it was Jake who refused to talk about painful subjects—"let's shut up about it," he tells Brett; now it is Brett who exclaims, "Don't let's ever talk about it. Please don't let's ever talk about it." When Brett came to Jake's apartment Jake "lay face down on the bed" because he "did not want to see her"; when Jake comes to Brett's hotel room in Madrid it is Brett who "would not look up." In Madrid Brett does the crying that Jake had done in Paris.

What accounts for the radically altered nature of their relationship is that Jake, not Brett, has changed. Brett's greeting to Jake—"Darling! I've had such a hell of a time" —duplicates her earlier "Oh, darling, I've been so miserable." Her lack of self-control in Madrid—"How can I help it?" she asks Jake—corresponds to her previously having told Jake, "I can't help it. I've never been able to help anything." Rather than Brett, it is Jake who has changed and, thanks to the example of Pedro Romero and his self-renewal at San Sebastian, changed dramatically. . . .

JAKE DRINKS TO WIN

After Jake and Brett leave the Hotel Montana for cocktails and lunch, Jake's words and acts continue to demonstrate his emotional independence of Brett. When Brett tells Jake to think about her having already been attending school in Paris at the time Romero was born, Jake responds with humor and detachment: "Anything you want me to think about it?" Moreover, Jake metaphorically separates himself from Brett through his statements and conduct. When Brett asserts that "deciding not to be a bitch" is "what we have instead of God," Jake challenges her use of the plural pronoun: "Some people have God. . . . Quite a lot." During lunch their emotional separation is further implied by Jake's eating "a very big meal" while Brett, like the sick and defeated Belmonte, eats very little. For the first time in the novel Jake feels "fine" while he is with Brett. He is now able to integrate the lessons of Count Mippipopolous and Pedro Romero, getting his money's worth of life's pleasures in a pressure-packed situation. Like the Count, he can now "enjoy everything so well" because through experience he has gotten to know the values. "I like to do a lot of things," Jake twice tells Brett. Like Romero, he can dominate his bull; it is Jake rather than Brett who controls the action, selecting the restaurant where they dine and deciding to take a carriage ride through Madrid.

Jake's drinking a good deal of wine does not mean, as Brett believes, that he is trying to drown his frustrations in alcohol. In Pamplona Jake may have gotten drunk to "Get over [his] damn depression," but this is a changed Jake. He drinks, as he explains, because he finds it enjoyable. Metaphorically, Jake drinks heavily to drive home the utter necessity of complete emotional severance from Brett, which is yet to come. Through the use of juxtaposition—in Paris Brett had told Jake that he was "slow on the up-take," but in Madrid it is Jake who says, "You haven't drunk much"—Hemingway again underlines the reversal in their relationship. As Brett and Jake are about to leave the restaurant Jake says, "I'll finish this," a remark meaningful on at least three levels. Jake's draining his glass first indicates that he will not leave a mess behind him which he or others must later clean up. Second, by finishing his drink Jake makes sure of getting his money's worth of wine, just as he is now getting his money's worth of enjoyment from life. Finally, "I'll finish this" conveys Jake's intention of permanently ending his romantic relationship with Brett.

JAKE'S FINAL TEST

The final and crucial test which Jake must pass before his victory is assured begins when he and Brett emerge from the coolness of the restaurant into the "hot and bright" streets of Madrid. Previously, Jake had always conducted himself well in the shaded and breezy settings of Bayonne, Burguete, and San Sebastian, but in the heat of Paris and Pamplona his self-control had been lost. This time, however, Jake is master of himself and the situation. In contrast to the first taxi ride in Paris, Jake does not ask Brett where she would like to drive but instead chooses their destination himself, again signaling a reversal from their earlier positions but more importantly signifying that Jake knows exactly the direction in which he must proceed if he is to "finish this." As the taxi starts Jake is relaxed and confident. He sits "comfortably" even when Brett rests her body against his. He does not stare at Brett as he had during the first ride or as the steers had stared at the bull. In fact, the cab ride in Madrid more closely resembles Jake's *fiacre* ride with the prostitute Georgette than the earlier drive with Brett. When Jake had gotten into the *fiacre* with Georgette he had "settled back" until, as he relates, "She cuddled against me and I put my arm around her." This sequence of events is duplicated in Madrid. Having "settled back" in the taxi, Jake explains that "Brett moved close to me" and "I put my arm around her. . . ." The point is that Brett no more dominates Jake in the present that Georgette had in the past.

When the taxi turns onto the "Gran Via," Jake and Brett are on the "great way," the symbolic highway of life. Their responses, therefore, will reveal with high accuracy their current attitude toward each other and to life:

> "Oh, Jake," Brett said, "we could have had such a damned good time together."

Brett's remark is obviously inspired by self-pity. Since her affair with Romero has turned out badly—although Brett claims she made Romero leave, her crying and trembling together with her refusal to "look up" indicate that, as in Pamplona, she "couldn't hold him"—she seems to have no alternative but to go back to Mike who, she honestly admits, is her "sort of thing." But Brett wishes it were otherwise, and her feeling sorry for herself prompts her remark, aimed as it is both to rationalize her own failings by blaming circumstance and to evoke from Jake the sympathy and compassion she feels entitled to.

Jake, by contrast, refuses to indulge in self-pity or to share her illusions:

> Ahead was a mounted policeman in khaki directing traffic. He raised his baton. The car slowed suddenly pressing Brett against me.

> "Yes," I said. "Isn't it pretty to think so?"

In the closing line of the novel Jake suggests . . . that it is foolish to believe, even had there been no war wound, that he and Brett could ever "have had such a damned good time together." But although critic Mark Spilka properly recognizes the military and phallic references in the "mounted policeman in khaki" and the "raised . . . baton," his conclusion that war and society have made true love impossible for those of Jake's generation oversimplifies the psychological subtleties of the situation. The reference to the khaki-clad policeman and his erect baton functions primarily to create for Jake the circumstances under which he would be most likely to revert to his old self, to lose control and to allow Brett once again to dominate him. Jake passes the ultimate and severest test of his newly won manhood by resisting the temptation, as Brett could not, to blame the failure of their relationship upon the war or his sexual incapacity. Under maximum pressure, created physically and emotionally by Brett's "pressing . . . against" him, Jake delivers in his final words the *coup de grâce* which effectively and permanently destroys all possibilities for the continuation of a romantic liaison between them.

Paris and the Characters of *The Sun Also Rises*

David Morgan Zehr

David Morgan Zehr, an assistant professor of English at the University of Alabama, contrasts the way Jake Barnes perceives Paris and how the rest of the expatriates perceive the city, which in Hemingway's day was considered an economical Shangri-la of beauty, culture, and partying by the Americans who fled there. Jake is the only character who enjoys Paris for its own sake, as a complex city rather than a tourist attraction. Zehr suggests that this is why the others rely so heavily on him as their resident oracle.

When Ernest Hemingway wrote *The Sun Also Rises* it was a significant thematic and personal choice to set the first third of the novel in Paris. It was in the fabled Paris of the 1920s that Hemingway had served his literary apprenticeship and written his first novel; yet during the 1920s the very name of Paris had come to suggest a world of debauchery, irresponsibility, and escapism—in fact, the whole idea of an expatriated lost generation with which Hemingway himself had become popularly identified. But while Paris was transformed by many into a kind of malignant Sodom and Gomorrah that was sapping the moral strength of a generation, it was being equally mythified by those who came to Paris to find and create a romanticized Bohemia free from the social and moral constrictions of home and to enjoy the long party while it lasted. *The Sun Also Rises,* however, neither confirms nor falls victim to such easy generalizations; the Paris it depicts is neither a romanticized Utopia nor an immoral Babylon. Instead Hemingway attempts to correct and set in perspective such imaginative conceptions by presenting an extensive critical portrait of expatriates and their reasons for being in

Excerpted from "Paris and the Expatriate Mystique: Hemingway's *The Sun Also Rises*," by David Morgan Zehr. Reprinted from *Arizona Quarterly*, vol. 33, no. 2 (1977), by permission of the Regents of the University of Arizona.

Paris and by showing that the expatriate Jake Barnes is not aimlessly drifting like so many others, but that he has a job which he enjoys and that he has a sensitive awareness and appreciation of a physical, non-Americanized Paris—a city of streets, buildings, cafés, and common people. The first third of *The Sun Also Rises*, then, is a meticulous and balanced process of clarifying and defining the relationship between the mystique of the expatriate and the city of Paris, and this in turn enables Hemingway to implicitly justify his own presence in Paris as a working, producing expatriate.

While Jake Barnes's appreciation for Paris and Robert Cohn's incapacity to enjoy Paris represent the central conflict of opposing expatriate attitudes, Hemingway also depicts a pervasive "expatriate consciousness" that underlies the Parisian milieu. This theme begins with the first meeting between Jake and Robert Cohn. Having grown bored with the limited and restricted life of the expatriate colony, Cohn dreams of going to a romanticized South America. Jake's advice to him points out the failure of many expatriates to recognize the reality of Paris: "This is a good town. Why don't you start living your life in Paris?" The idea that many are unable to adapt to Paris without associating mainly with other Americans and creating an American atmosphere is suggested early in the novel by a brief but significant scene. When Jake and the prostitute Georgette drive by the New York *Herald* Bureau office, Georgette notices that the window is full of clocks: "What are all the clocks for?" she asks; and Jake tells her, "They show the hour all over America." It is precisely such details as this that inform the underlying expatriate consciousness. America still has the "correct" time, and these clocks offer a comforting confirmation of the presence of America for those who remain fundamentally detached from their immediate environment.

PARIS, THE AMUSEMENT PARK

At Braddocks's *bal musette* Hemingway continues to show the widespread superficiality of both the tourists' and the expatriates' response to Paris. Robert Prentiss, a young American novelist with a cultivated British accent, asks Jake, "Do you find Paris amusing?" The very word "amusing" suggests Prentiss's insubstantial response to Paris. A similar opening question occurs when Count Mippipopolous first meets Lady Brett Ashley: "Well, does your Ladyship have a good time here in Paris?" As a refuge from the outside world, a vacation spot, Paris is a place to be "amused" and to "have a good time"; and this further suggests the limited and detached manner of the expatriate's response to Paris. This idea is particularly clarified in the encounter between Robert Cohn's mistress, Frances, and the prostitute Georgette. Frances's opening question is similar to the previous two, suggesting a link in sensibility that binds foreigners together: "You love Paris, do you not?" But Georgette is a Parisian "worker," not an expatriate or a tourist, and so replies, "No, I don't like Paris. It is expensive and dirty." The conflict here is clearly between one who is a part of this city—who lives and works there—and one who has formed her own limited conception of Paris at Americanized bars in Montparnasse. And it is just such self-assured but essentially superficial "tourist" responses that Hemingway is implicitly dissociating from Jake Barnes's more complex relationship to Paris. . . .

JAKE THE PARISIAN

For Jake Barnes . . . Paris represents neither an amusing diversion, nor a substitute for an American city, nor an anesthetic to his own personal malaise. Instead, we receive through Jake's consciousness a rounded, affectionate portrait of a physical Paris populated by Parisians as well as other nationalities. The precarious balance that Jake maintains between his public and private worlds is strikingly unique in the novel and results from three general characteristics. First, while Jake inhabits the milieu of the expatriate, he manages to avoid becoming limited or defined by an "expatriate club." Second, Jake's office, representing a place of work and accomplishment, stands in vivid contrast to the mythified idea of Paris as a dissipating playground. And third, in his walks through the city Jake gives concrete, particularized descriptions of Paris and thus reveals a recognition and acceptance of a natural, energetic city of great physical charm.

For Jake to maintain himself on the periphery of the expatriate milieu he must balance a public involvement with a private independence. At Braddocks's *bal musette* Jake knows almost everyone there, but does not appear to be a regular member; involved with a world that proved to be a source for Hemingway's art, Jake, like Hemingway, does not surrender or abandon himself to this world but maintains a carefully modulated psychological distance. On his way home after leaving the party Jake notes that "across the street at the Dome . . . Some one waved at me from a table, I did not see who it was and went on. I wanted to get home." This anonymous character suggests a world of vaguely familiar faces that form an "expatriate colony" which Jake acknowledges but does not depend upon for his identity. And later, when Bill Gorton and Jake go to Madame Lecomte's restaurant for dinner, they find it crowded with Americans: "Some one had put it in the American Women's Club list as a quaint restaurant on the Paris quais as yet untouched by Americans. . . ." The impression from this incident is that American tourists have violated the essential value of the restaurant by opening up the possibility of its becoming another Dome or Rotonde. When Madame Lecomte asks Jake why he never comes there anymore, Jake honestly replies, "Too many compatriots."

We are also conscious of Jake's uniqueness in this milieu as a man with a job. When he runs into Woolsey and Krum it is after "a good morning's work" and occurs while Jake is covering a news conference. We see Jake actually at work in his office, while Robert Cohn sleeps on his couch. On the way to work one morning Jake thinks how "It felt pleasant to be going to work." And, what may be a further attempt by Hemingway to clarify his own life in Paris, Jake modifies the fact of his work by maintaining an image of himself as unpressured by the responsibilities of his job. When Robert Cohn interrupts him at his job, it is Jake who suggests they go for a drink; and when Cohn asks, "Aren't you working?" Jake simply replies, "No." But Jake reveals that this is only a ploy; after a drink he intends to excuse himself in order to send some cables, and he will have thus freed himself for more work while maintaining the illusion of easy availability: "It is very important to discover graceful exits like that in the newspaper business, where it is such an important part of the ethics that you should never seem to be working." If we substitute the "writing business" for the "newspaper business," Jake becomes a clarification of Hemingway's own life of work and discipline amidst the café society and bohemian atmosphere of Paris with which he was popularly identified.

The third characteristic that clearly differentiates Jake from his compatriots is his consciousness of Paris itself; throughout the first third of *The Sun Also Rises* Jake's descriptions of a physical, substantial Paris are counterpointed against the insubstantial, created images of Paris of those who find there no more than a superficial reflection of themselves and their expectations. Jake is the only character who has a rounded conception of Paris; and he implicitly condemns the mythifying of the city by revealing a physical, nonglamorized Paris—a Paris filled with street names, trees, statues, parks, a river full of active barges, and common people viably involved in the daily life of the city.

When Robert Cohn complains to Jake about his boredom with Paris and the Latin Quarter, Jake tells him: "This is a good town. . . . Stay away from the Quarter. Cruise around by yourself and see what happens to you." And after Cohn admits that he did wander around one night, and Jake asks him, "Wasn't the town nice at night?" Cohn only replies, "I don't care for Paris." Cohn's failure is a failure of sensibility, and his inability to transcend the limiting expatriate world of Paris contrasts with Jake's sensitive appreciation of the physical city. One of Jake's many particularized descriptions of Paris occurs the morning after Braddocks's party:

> It was a fine morning. The horse-chestnut trees in the Luxembourg gardens were in bloom. . . . The flower-women were coming up from the market and arranging their daily stock. Students went by going up to the law school, or down to the Sorbonne. The Boulevard was busy with trams and people going to work. . . . I passed the man with the jumping frogs and the man with the boxer toys. . . . I walked on behind a man who was pushing a roller that printed the name CINZANO on the sidewalk in damp letters. All along people were going to work. It felt pleasant to be going to work.

Because of such unaffected, often lyrical descriptions the reader implicitly understands that Jake Barnes is neither an intruder nor a violator of Paris. Instead the reader recognizes that Jake fits naturally into the environment and that his knowledge and awareness of Paris is broader and more sensitive than that of his compatriots. Through Jake's eyes we become conscious of a Paris separate from that of the Americanized bars of Montparnasse, a world neither limited nor adulterated by an expatriate consciousness:

> Crossing the Seine I saw a string of barges being towed empty down the current, riding high, the bargemen at the sweeps as they came toward the bridge. The river looked nice. It was always pleasant crossing bridges in Paris.

And the fact that all of these descriptions occur when Jake is alone, with the single exception of one that occurs with Bill Gorton, emphasizes the nature of his private life and the quality of his sensibility—even though at the same time he might be on his way to the Select or the Dome. By suggesting that Paris is not just a glamorous, sensual Arcadia, but that it is an intensely alive, energetic, and beautiful city, and thus a fruitful environment for work, Hemingway continues to justify his own presence in Paris and to qualify the mystique of both the dissipated expatriate and a Babylonian Paris.

While people like Robert Cohn have an "incapacity to enjoy Paris" and others seek temporary anesthetics through sensation and experience, Jake Barnes maintains a balance between his participation in this expatriate world and his private consciousness. And the fact that Jake's involvement with this "expatriate colony" is counterpointed by both his work and his nonsentimentalized descriptions of Paris suggests a carefully interwoven process by which Hemingway was able to neutralize the popular myths of his own life in Paris. By the end of the Paris section we understand that Paris is far from being a decadent trap that has dissipated either the journalist Jake Barnes or the writer Ernest Hemingway.

Finally, it is significant that it is not until they are out of Paris and in Spain that Bill Gorton ironically labels Jake with his oft quoted description:

> You're an expatriate. You've lost touch with the soil. You get precious. Fake European standards have ruined you. You drink yourself to death. You become obsessed by sex. You spend all your time talking, not working. You are an expatriate, see?

The full ironic force of this statement could not have been appreciably felt before they had left Paris and Hemingway had been able to give a rounded portrait of Americans and expatriates in Paris. The statement clearly fits many of Jake's compatriots, but it is just this kind of overly generalized mystique of the lost generation that the first third of *The Sun Also Rises* implicitly condemns. By this point in the novel we have gained an informed perspective and are able to judge for ourselves the inaccuracy of such a popular, unqualified generalization—for we have realized that living in Paris is a more complex experience than a simple escape into a contemporary Babylon or Bohemia.

Confused Chronology in *The Sun Also Rises*

J.F. Kobler

The chronology of Hemingway's sequence of historical events is not accurate, according to Hemingway pundit and North Texas State University professor of English J.F. Kobler. Here he shows that Hemingway, arguably the most exacting prose stylist in modern times and a former newspaper reporter himself, demonstrates little accuracy with regard to his timeline. Kobler ultimately contends that it is unlikely these breaches are intentional.

Although Jake Barnes' chronicle of the vacation trip he and his friends took from Paris to Pamplona appears to be precise and accurate in all details, actually the days and dates provided in *The Sun Also Rises* are totally confused. Also, the dates of two actual events are inaccurately used by Hemingway in this novel.

Jake and Bill's departure from Paris, their one-night stopovers in Bayonne and Pamplona, their fishing in the Irati River, and the entire group's participation in the festival at Pamplona take place within a time span established by two explicitly stated dates and days of the week. Jake tells us no less than three times that he and Bill Gorton plan to leave Paris on June 25. Mike Campbell even asks what day of the week that is, and someone, apparently Jake, tells him that it is a Saturday. Jake later recounts a conversation with Brett Ashley which took place on "the night of the 24th of June." He then explains in the following narrative paragraphs that "Bill and I took the morning train from the Gare d'Orsay." Unquestionably, then, the trip began on June 25, a Saturday in Hemingway's chronology. At the other end of the vacation, Jake says specifically that "At noon of Sunday, the 6th of July, the fiesta exploded."

Excerpted from "Confused Chronology in *The Sun Also Rises*," by J.F. Kobler, *Modern Fiction Studies*, vol. 13, no. 4 (1967–1968), pp. 517–20; © Purdue Research Foundation. Reprinted by permission of the Johns Hopkins University Press.

It has long been assumed that the action of this novel occurs in 1925, because that is the year Hemingway, his first wife Hadley, and some of their friends made a similar trip together to Pamplona for the *Feria de San Fermin*. And Hemingway started writing the novel almost immediately after that trip, on his birthday, July 21, 1925, "while recent events were still fresh in his mind," as [author Carlos] Baker puts it. Also, the two previously mentioned actual events did take place in 1925, although their precise dates in that year are used incorrectly in the novel, as I shall show later. However, in 1925, June 25 was not a Saturday (it was a Thursday), and July 6 was not a Sunday, but a Monday.

Even if this action is supposed to occur in some year other than 1925, it is impossible for June 25 to be a Saturday and July 6, a Sunday. There are ten days between those two dates, not the right number to get from any Saturday to any Sunday in any year. So something is basically wrong with Jake's account.

THE "MISSING" WEEK

The following day-by-day summary of this account shows both the nature and extent of the other errors in chronology. As already noted, Jake and Bill take the morning train from Paris, as planned, on Saturday, June 25. They ride all day, getting into Bayonne at "about nine o'clock" that night. The next day (June 26) they rent a car because the bus does not start running until July 1 and drive to Pamplona, where they spend that night in the Hotel Montoya. Jake reports that "In the morning [Monday, June 27] I bought three tickets for the bus to Burguete." Robert Cohn, who met Jake and Bill in Pamplona, decides not to go on the fishing trip, but the other two leave after lunch that same day "to go to Burguete." They arrive in that town late in the day and take rooms at an inn.

The next morning (Tuesday, June 28, by Jake's reckoning) they walk out to the Irati for their first day of fishing. Although Jake describes specifically and in detail only this one day of fishing, he does say, "We stayed five days at Burguete and had good fishing."

Right after reporting on the length of their stay in Burguete, Jake tells about receiving a letter from Mike dated "San Sebastian, Sunday." This letter says that Mike and Brett are planning to "go to Montoya Hotel Pamplona Tuesday." Jake gets this letter on a Wednesday, a fact precisely established when he asks the Englishman Harris what day of the week it is. When he is told it is a Wednesday, Jake comments, "We've been here nearly a week." Obviously, it is impossible for Jake and Bill to have "stayed five days at Burguete" or to have been there "nearly a week" and the day be only Wednesday, June 29. They left Paris on June 25 and spent three days getting to Burguete. Nor can this particular Wednesday be the following one, July 6 on any normal calendar. Besides, according to Jake's calendar July 6 was a Sunday.

In addition to this confusion, further contradiction is evident in the letter in regard to Mike and Brett's activities during this time. The letter reads, "We got here [San Sebastian] Friday." But as noted earlier, Jake tells about talking to Brett in Paris on the night of Friday, June 24, making it rather difficult for her to have arrived in San Sebastian that same day.

Meanwhile, back on the Irati, Jake and Bill get ready to leave and go back into Pamplona on Wednesday, whatever date in June or July it happens to be. On this particular Wednesday, they join the others in Pamplona and they all inspect some of the incoming bulls and engage in other assorted activities. Just before supper that night Jake and Bill talk about the immediate future: "To-morrow [Thursday] come the Miuras," bulls from a particular breeding ranch, and the fiesta itself begins "day after to-morrow," or Friday. But shortly after this conversation Jake says that "The next two days in Pamplona were quiet" as the "town was getting ready for the fiesta." If the fiesta began on Friday, then it was not likely a quiet day. The reader also wonders what happened to that intervening Saturday.

THE TWO HISTORICAL GAFFES

In addition to creating this confusion with his fictional chronology, Hemingway also mentions two actual events whose dates can be easily ascertained. Both are wrong in the novel. Just before telling of his plans to leave Paris on June 25, Jake says that "The Ledoux–Kid Francis fight was the night of the 20th of June." Actually, the fight was on June 9. The following is the first sentence of an Associated Press story datelined Paris, June 9, and appearing in the June 10, 1925, New York *Times:* "Young Kid Francis, a bantamweight who learned to box in Argentina, tonight defeated the veteran Charles Ledoux, former bantamweight champion of Europe in a 12-round bout."

The second erroneous historical reference concerns the date of the death of William Jennings Bryan. During their first day of fishing on the Irati, Jake tells Bill that Bryan just died, "I read it in the paper yesterday." Now this date is, according to Jake's account, June 28, but Bryan died on July 26, 1925, almost exactly a month later. If the year of the novel is 1925 or earlier, Jake's newspaper was doing an amazing job; if the time is 1926 or later, Jake was slow getting around to reading his papers.

The date of the opening of the *Feria de San Fermín,* in contrast, is correct in the novel. It always begins on July 6. And July 6 was a Sunday in 1924, but not in 1925. Perhaps the fact that Hemingway also participated in the San Fermín rites in 1923 and 1924 accounts for part of the confusion in the novel. The memories of three trips blended together to create the fictional events.

ACCIDENT OR DESIGN?

Still the question remains, did Hemingway create this chronological confusion on purpose or did he fall into it accidentally because of more than one visit to Pamplona? If it was done on purpose, his intentions may have been either external or internal to the novel. One rather dubious external reason might involve some intention of throwing off readers as to the autobiographical nature of the book, to confuse the issue about the year being the one in which Hemingway and his friends made their corresponding visit to Spain. If so, he failed. The confusion in dates has gone unnoticed, but the real people behind these fictitious characters have long been recognized. Nor does it make much sense for an author to throw in two historical dates from 1925 (even though they are slightly wrong) if he is trying to camouflage the year. I cannot believe that such confusion was his intention. Nor do I believe that Hemingway was simply playing a joke on his readers, testing them to see if they would discover the mixup. Hemingway did not use such practical jokes in his fiction. He took his art much too seriously to play around with it this way.

If the reason for the muddled dates is internal, then the confusion must say something about Jake Barnes' character. Since the novel is Jake's first person story, the reader may lay the confusion to him rather than to the author. Such a chronological mixup might indicate that Jake as narrator is forgetful, confused, or emotionally disturbed. Of these three possibilities, Jake falls only remotely into the last category. His inability to consummate his love for Brett is obviously an emotionally disturbing factor. Like most principal male characters in Hemingway's works, however, Jake reveals this disturbance only at night in the quiet of his own bedroom. This is not to say that his emotions could not be shown in other ways, such as through confusion in his narration. But Hemingway in no other instance in this novel even hints at such weaknesses in Jake's emotional stability. In fact, it is he to whom all the other and weaker characters turn for advice and leadership. Critics through the years have consistently seen Jake Barnes as the strongest figure in this novel. It will take more than evidence of this chronological confusion to change their minds about the basic strengths of this character. Also, his job as newspaper correspondent ought to be evidence of his ability to keep facts and dates straight.

Therefore, I must conclude that these chronological errors are not purposeful, but accidental. Hemingway simply did not go back and check his facts after creating a chronicle out of three personal visits to Pamplona. The mistakes are understandable, but not forgiveable. Probably he and his editors did not hold a calendar up to those dates because the account has such seeming exactness and so many precise details that it was assumed to be accurate. Readers and critics for more than forty years have been lulled into the same kind of automatic acceptance by the apparent preciseness of the account.

CHAPTER 2

Characters in *The Sun Also Rises*

READINGS ON
THE SUN ALSO RISES

The Character of Robert Cohn

Robert E. Meyerson

Noted Hemingway scholar Robert E. Meyerson finds
that Robert Cohn's presence strengthens the novel's
sentimental theme. Cohn is resented and treated
harshly by the rest for being untouched by the war
and for remaining idealistic. His Jewishness only of-
fends them more in that it entitles him to the trophy
of a world-class "sufferer" who in reality has never
experienced true tragedy, as they have. So they make
him pay.

[Holocaust scholar] Hannah Arendt, in her brilliant analysis
of anti-Semitism, that "outrage to common sense" as she so
aptly characterizes it, recounts the old story about the anti-
Semite who claims that the Jews caused the First World War.
"Yes," his foil replies, "the Jews and the bicyclists." "Why the
bicyclists?" asks the anti-Semite. "Why the Jews?" responds
the foil.

Arendt tells this old joke in order to introduce us to the
scapegoat theory of anti-Semitism, a theory which she not
only cracks but rather demolishes by way of explaining the
role of anti-Semitism in the theory and practice of National
Socialism. Basically, Arendt argues that the anti-Semites did
not take aim at the Jews arbitrarily, as the facetious foil of
the joke does in order to make his point and as the scapegoat
theorists do in order to make theirs. Rather, the anti-Semites
chose their Jewish target quite deliberately as a means, first,
of facilitating the destruction of the old European state system and, second, of introducing their new method of political rule: terror. Annihilation of the Jews and of traditional
political life went hand in hand for the particular reasons
whose skeletal history Arendt records.

Of course, the historical fallout radiating from Arendt's

Excerpted from "Why Robert Cohn? An Analysis of Hemingway's *The Sun Also Rises*,"
by Robert E. Meyerson, *The Liberal and Fine Arts Review*, vol. 2, no. 1 (1982). Reprinted
with permission of Eastern New Mexico University.

analysis with all its implications of ideology, Nazism, terror, and genocide has nothing to do with Ernest Hemingway. But Arendt's suggestion that anti-Semitism in politics must be regarded as rational, as deliberately chosen, at least for the lessons it hopes to impart, has much to do with Hemingway and with a proper understanding of his first great success, *The Sun Also Rises.* It would be all too easy to write off Hemingway's portrait of the Jew Robert Cohn as an inconsequential by-product of a then-fashionable upper middle-class anti-Semitism or as a fictional insult aimed at a real-life model. . . .

Responding to a chiding Communist-admirer, Ivan Kashkeen, Hemingway archly confessed: "I believe in only one thing: liberty. . . . I believe in the absolute minimum of government. . . . A true work of art endures forever; no matter what its politics." And that was that. Hemingway, for all his scoffing at academic and philosophic critics, was sufficiently irritated by his Communist critic to fashion a crude philosophical tool to help him work his way out of the unjust criticism of being socially irresponsible. But his senses were not so pained as to make him try his hand "at a sustained theory of art and politics—after all, Hemingway was the kind of artist who regards criticism as just another form of parasitism." If he could draw a one-paragraph distinction between the two without sacrificing the one to the other, he felt he had done quite enough. Politically speaking, his position was classically liberal, and, so far as his belief in liberty signified a respect for the value of political life rather than an anarchistic and therefore sentimental rejection of the value of all political action, many will agree that Hemingway's judgment was sound. But even if we do not grant Hemingway the benefit of the doubt, we must concede that anarchism is scarcely compatible with fascism—nihilism, perhaps, but anarchism most definitely not.

If Hemingway's judgment of the relationship between art and politics was basically sound, or at any rate anti-ideological, how then do we explain the fact of Robert Cohn? . . .

To be precise, Cohn's role in the unfolding plot is actually that of a strong accompanist helping to underscore the piece played by the leading men and the primadonna. On the one hand, Cohn is the negative to the picture of Hemingway's unabashedly perfect hero, the bullfighter Pedro Romero.

Where Pedro enters the story to the instant acclaim of a Hemingway gang impressed by his great looks and relentless potential, Cohn is introduced in terms of a dubious badge-of-courage broken nose and a rather pathetic insistence on cultivating his meager literary talents. Where Pedro is all grace and effectiveness in the bull ring and in front of his numerous admirers, Cohn is a cloying pest stumbling around a circle of nauseated fellow expatriates. Where Pedro stoically endures and even masters the physical pain suffered at Cohn's skillful fists by proceeding to triumph over the menacing bull, lending his life meaning and accomplishment, Cohn mawkishly opens up his psychological wounds for public display until at last he fades out of view and into oblivion. If on the one hand Cohn therefore helps to set off the true picture of heroism, on the other hand he helps bring out the worst in the group of lost souls whose depths only seem to well up in the service of some small-time decadent purpose, such as Bill's impetuous and ill-advised bet regarding the time of Brett's arrival in Pamplona or Mike's accelerating cuckold rage resulting in an overturned dinner-laden table. Cohn thus proves to be both a bad example and a bad influence. Or, as Allen Tate put it in the heat of his first impressions as book reviewer for *The Nation* in 1926, "Robert Cohn [is] a most offensive cad."

THE "REAL" COHN

But if Cohn's function in Hemingway's tale is clear, what is not so clear is the purpose of rendering Cohn a Jew. To be sure, Cohn, like all the characters in the novel, is based on a real-life individual, Harold Loeb. Loeb, like Robert Cohn, was the scion of rich New York Jewish families, a Princeton graduate, a formidable boxer and tennis player, a dabbler in affairs literary, and a short-lived lover of Lady Duff Twysden, the real-life woman model for Hemingway's Lady Ashley. Like Cohn, Loeb sneaked off with his Duff Twysden / Lady Ashley just as he was scheduled to fish in Spain with Hemingway and other friends. Many of the melodramatic details of this real-life tryst and the subsequent regrouping during the holiday approximate those related in *The Sun Also Rises*, even to the extent of the falling-out between Barnes and Cohn, with the exception that in real life the fight between Hemingway and Loeb ended by mutual consent without a blow having been struck, whereas in the novel Jake gets knocked on his prat. While both Hemingway's biographer, Carlos Baker, and Loeb himself record the fact that Hemingway and Duff Twysden were drawn to each other, neither seems to think that anything much came of it. . . .

CONSTANT "JEWISH" REFERENCES

Appositive and parenthetical-like allusions to Cohn's Jewishness and Jews in general are numerous, indeed all too numerous in *The Sun Also Rises.* Early in the story, narrator Jake Barnes sets the tone by snorting out his disgust over his inability to deflect Cohn from an ill-conceived plan to travel to South America: "He had a hard, Jewish, stubborn streak." Later, Jake takes a humorous poke at Cohn by describing his impressions of Cohn's first glimpse of Lady Ashley: "He looked a great deal as his compatriot must have looked when he saw the promised land." The other characters follow suit. Bill Gorton and Mike Campbell frequently raise the Jewish question throughout the novel:

BILL TO JAKE: "Well, let him not get superior and Jewish."

BILL TO JAKE: "Haven't you got some more Jewish friends you could bring along?"

MIKE TO JAKE: "No, listen, Jake. Brett's gone off with men. But they weren't ever Jews, and they didn't come and hang about afterward."

BILL TO JAKE: "He's got this Jewish superiority so strong that he thinks the only emotion he'll get out of the fight will be being bored."

MIKE TO JAKE: "I gave Brett what for, you know. I said if she would go about with Jews and bullfighters and such people, she must expect trouble."

Even Brett finally learns how to play the game when, in exasperation, she refers to "that damned Jew" by way of trying to evoke sympathy from the ever compliant Jake. This list, while not exhaustive, is sufficiently tedious to make the point. But the tedium is Hemingway's characters'; it is not accidental. Hemingway was far too meticulous and demanding a craftsman for all this anti-Semitism to be accidental.

For the most part, references to Cohn's Jewishness or to Jews in general are just the mindless pot shots of trigger-happy loose tongues. The impetus behind them is not specific. They do not serve to convey information about Cohn or Jews. Rather, they are a measure of the mood of the characters who utter them. They are also another indication of the abandonment of that polite social pretense that these honest casualties of the Great War can no longer abide, a measure of the gone-to-seed indulgence of a generation without values, a generation with only its personal pleasures and pains. Novel hero Jake Barnes, while sharing in much of this bitter convalescing, nevertheless does try to get hold of himself—his return to San Sebastian and vigorous swimming toward the end of the story may be understood not so much as the cold shower that cools down his passion for Brett, nor the baptism that washes away his sins in order to open up the opportunity for new life but, rather, as the conscious effort to break through the syndrome of drunkenness and boorishness that characterizes the expatriate fling in Pamplona. Of course, Brett's emergency telegram quickly pulls Jake back into the suicidal world of his peers, thus undermining the possibility of his fully breaking with fate. But Jake never foreswears the possibility of salvaging something from his life, only the reverie that things might be fundamentally different. Given this aesthetic / moral dialectic that plays itself out within Jake's soul—a struggle between his better, because intentional, but emasculated self and his indulgent, because irresolute, but also passively resigned self—Jake's expressions of anti-Semitism and occasional enjoyment of Cohn's discomfiture may well be regarded as the antithesis to his more sober and balanced moments. Indeed, just before the stormy fiesta is to begin and just after a fresh and cool evening rain has calmed all nerves, Jake as narrator tells us: "We all felt good and we felt healthy, and I felt quite friendly to Cohn." Thus attitudes toward Cohn rise and fall according to the health and welfare of those around him. This, as well as those several instances, more numerous in the early pages, where Jake the narrator describes Cohn's virtues and likeable traits, is the best evidence for Hemingway's contention, seconded by one critic who reads into Robert Cohn a restrained heroism, that "If you think the book is anti-Semitic you must be out of your mind. . . ."

But the fact that Cohn is not a complete villain and the fact that he has his better moments does not mean that he thereby joins the ranks of Hemingway's heroes. And the fact that Cohn serves as a barometer of the moral health of the novel's cast of characters does not mean that he himself is without further significance. Indeed, it is this very quality of

Cohn's as human lightning rod, as the salient figure who draws the vicious energies out of a charged social environment, which leads us to the more likely explanation of Hemingway's purpose in including a Jew as a key figure in this work. Two of the more articulate references to Cohn and Jewishness are especially telling. In one, Mike Campbell speaks of the heavy interest payments that Brett must make to her creditors, "to Jews." But then he immediately sets the record straight by adding, "They're not really Jews. We just call them Jews. They're Scotsmen, I believe." The reader is unequivocally informed that the matter of alleged Jewish niggardliness and Shylockian business practice is not at stake here. The real issue, however, is revealed when Brett officially divests herself of the last trace of consideration for Cohn and figuratively bares her breast: "I hate him, too. . . . I hate his damned suffering."

Admittedly, there is no specific mention of Cohn's Jewishness here. But by this point in the story there is no need for it. Cohn has been coupled with the designation so often that the two, Cohn and Jew, become inseparable. It is Cohn's suffering as the particular manifestation of a more generalized Jewish characteristic that Hemingway is after. And by the time Brett confesses that she is sick of it, the reader is ready to agree with her.

Why Cohn Offends the Rest

Suffering is an issue of major proportions in *The Sun Also Rises*. It is the source of the initial problem of the book: how can Jake Barnes, veteran of the First World War, try to fashion a life for himself as a writer in the face of the horrible wound he received in combat. That wound is, indeed, so basic that it need not even be described. Its consequences are clear, however: Jake is incapable of consummating the love he can still feel, like any other normally endowed male, for Lady Brett Ashley. Jake nevertheless does his best to detour his appetite by way of sport, as both participant and observer. He also tries to master his psychological and physical pain by detaching himself from the human involvement which would require either another disclosure of his problem or an abandonment of that easy simpering which substitutes for a facing-up to responsibility. In his negative moments, Jake, true to the model of the eunuch, is therefore eminently passive in his relationships with others. He does nothing to en-

courage or discourage the attentions of those he loves, like
Brett, those he often hates, like Cohn, or those for whom his
feelings are less pronounced, like Bill and Mike. At the same
time he obliges everyone, reconciled as he is to his role as
high priest officiating at the funeral service of a Lost Generation. If he can console Brett by pimping out a liaison with
the emotionally untried bullfighter, Pedro Romero, so be it; if
Cohn needs a shoulder to cry on, Jake obliges; if the boys
want another drinking partner, then Jake is their man. Jake's
mission is to minister to the incurable psychological wounds
of his generation, preferably with strong prescriptions of sex
and booze. Where the others are pathetic, however, Jake is
tragic; where the others have lost their nerve, Jake has lost
his manhood. All seem reconciled to their fate; all refuse to
damn their luck. Mike takes his bankruptcy without bitterness; Bill accepts his geographical buffeting-about as the way
of nature; Brett keeps trying out the fit of different masculine
replacement parts as a temporary surrogate for Jake. It is
only Robert Cohn who still believes in the possibility of a
happy ending and in his ability to effect it; only Cohn refuses
to believe that their brief love affair meant nothing to Brett;
only Cohn believes that the world should listen to his sad
lament; only Cohn refuses to find a substitute solution, insis-
tently acting as if fate had not fulfilled its part of the bargain,
as if the promised land of Lady Ashley were owed to him as
his part of the ancestral Covenant.

THE MARK OF THE LOST GENERATION

While all the expatriates in the book suffer, Cohn's case is
qualitatively different. All the expatriates with one exception
are veterans of the war. Even Brett qualifies by virtue of having lost her fiancée. The exception, of course, is Robert
Cohn—at least there is no mention of his war record (Harold
Loeb did serve in the United States Army during World War
I but never made it to the European front). It is this reason,
as much as any other, which lends deeper meaning to
Mike's taunting Cohn: "Do you think you belong here among
us? . . . Why don't you see when you're not wanted, Cohn?"
It is not only Cohn who is not wanted, but Jews in general,
as Mike indicates when describing the whole freakish affair
to Jake: "Brett's gone off with men. But they weren't ever
Jews. . . ." Brett at first tacitly, and later explicitly, agrees.
The veterans who fought on the winning side, who entered

the war hopefully and saw it through successfully, discover themselves to be losers after all, castrated like Jake, infertile like Brett, homeless like Bill, emotionally and financially bankrupt like Mike. Only Cohn, of all the central figures in the story, was unscathed by the most devastating war of all history to that date. Only Cohn refuses to acknowledge defeat after losing his personal battle for the love of Brett. More than Jake's admitted jealousy of Cohn's affair with Brett, it is Cohn's inability to comprehend and recognize tragedy that galls Hemingway / Barnes. The ultimate tragedy in the sense of the novel, of course, is that of an entire lost generation; and the ultimate jealousy is that of the Lost Generation for the champion sufferers of all time, the Jewish people.

Hemingway's book is both a celebration and a lament. What is celebrated is the loss of innocence, the pre-war innocence that still believed in ideals and covenants. What is lamented is the very same thing. It is this that constitutes Hemingway's sentimentality, his effort to paint a group portrait in colors both stylish and pathetic. It is, indeed, a sentimentality that would attempt the ultimate by raising its subject to the historical level, as indicated by the book's prefatory quotation from Ecclesiastes, the source of the book's title. However, there is one thing standing in the way of this apotheosis, and that is that the most coveted niche in the pantheon of suffering is already occupied by the all-time scapegoat: the Jewish people. Hemingway had to remove the Jewish bust from this niche in order to make room for his replacement: the Lost Generation.

As if to prove that the Lost Generation is the more worthy subject of historical sentimentality, Hemingway shows that its superiority lies in knowing when to accept defeat. By contrast, Robert Cohn and presumably the Jewish people as well never know when to quit. Indeed, the mark of the Lost Generation, as well as the Hemingway hero in general, is that only in defeat does it truly triumph: Jake Barnes and even Brett, by their unillusioned acceptance of the impossibility of consummated love; Frederic Henry and Robert Jordan by their successful completion of missions that end in personal disaster; Santiago the fisherman by his stubborn retaliation against an undoubtedly superior foe—it is as if true character is only achieved in the recognition of one's personal tragedy. Robert Cohn is the antithesis of such self-recognition. "What do you think it's meant to have that damned Jew about? . . ." Brett asks her Father Confessor Jake Barnes. It means that Robert Cohn and the Jewish people, with their illusions of Divine Favor and Divine Justice, refuse to go away and accept defeat gracefully and thereby clutter up everyone else's life. When they finally insist on causing a scene, Hemingway as the literary bouncer throws them out: Cohn, out of the story, and the Jews, out of history or at least out of their niche in the pantheon. By quoting from Ecclesiastes to the effect that "One generation passeth away, and another generation cometh; but the earth abideth forever, . . ." "Jesse James" Hemingway robs from the rich to give to the poor by stealing the epitaph from those who have outlived it and conferring it upon those who have most recently earned it. If it seems as if the suffering Jews contradict their prophet's moral by their longevity, they only do so relatively speaking in comparison with other, more short-lived, generational losers. But in comparison with the abiding earth, they too will pass away in the end.

In Defense of Brett

Roger Whitlow

Roger Whitlow is a professor of English at Eastern
Illinois University and the author of several books,
including *Black American Literature* and *Many Yan-
kee Faces.* In his book analyzing Hemingway's female
characters, *Cassandra's Daughters,* Whitlow argues
that Brett Ashley is simply a misunderstood victim of
bad press. In fact, when stacked against the behavior
of those vying for her affections, and considered in
the context of Hemingway's era and his personal
sensibilities, Brett's actions are at worst governed by
self-interest, but they are a far cry from bitchery.

Like other Hemingway heroines, Brett Ashley has been de-
nounced as a weak character. Allen Tate has called her
"false," and has claimed that she is more caricature than
character. Edwin Muir has claimed that Brett "is the senti-
mentally regarded dare-devil, and she never becomes real."
The more serious and frequent critical charges against Brett
Ashley, however, are that she lacks the characteristics of a
woman and, worse, that she is a "bitch." On the first charge,
Theodore Bardacke claims that Brett is a "woman devoid of
womanhood." Jackson Benson says that Brett is "a female
who never becomes a woman." Mimi Gladstein says that
Brett has a "bisexual image." And, the most pointed, Pamella
Farley calls Brett "a perversion of femininity." (Much has
been made lately, incidentally, based on "quick studies" of
Hemingway's unpublished manuscripts, of Hemingway's
own alleged bisexuality and general confusion of sex roles,
and, given the contemporary preoccupation with such matters, much more is surely going to be said about it.)

A careful reading of *The Sun Also Rises,* however—the
only one of his books that Hemingway was almost completely satisfied with—reveals that Brett was an individual
whose female sexual appeal and general attractiveness

Excerpted from *Cassandra's Daughters: The Women in Hemingway,* by Roger Whitlow.
Copyright © 1984 by Roger Whitlow. Reproduced with permission of Greenwood Publishing Group, Inc., Westport, CT.

were exceptional, despite her bobbed hair and her occasional association with homosexuals. From the beginning of the book, men find her irresistible. When Jake, as narrator, first introduces Brett, he says, "Brett was damned good-looking. She wore a slipover jersey sweater and a tweed skirt, and her hair was brushed back like a boy's. She started all that [that is, the new female hairstyle]. She was built with curves like the hull of a racing yacht, and you missed none of it with that wool jersey." Robert Cohn, too, is immediately captivated by Brett, and a short time later, he says, "She's a remarkably attractive woman."

Every significant male character in the novel at one time or another comments on Brett's female attractiveness. When he is introduced to Brett, Bill Gorton says, "Beautiful lady," and later he says, "She's damned nice." Mike Campbell says, "Brett, you *are* a lovely piece. Don't you think she's beautiful?"—a refrain that he reiterates through the rest of the novel. There are Jake's repeated narrative descriptions: "Brett wore a black, sleeveless evening dress. She looked quite beautiful" and "Brett was radiant" and, finally, the near-uncontrollable infatuation of the nineteen-year-old bullfighter, Pedro Romero, for Brett. Hemingway makes amply clear, in short, that this is an exceptionally appealing woman—bright, beautiful, and sexual—and to call Brett "nonfeminine," or "bisexual," or a "perversion of femininity," is to measure her by a standard of "womanhood" which is confining indeed.

BRETT'S BITCHERY

A more unfortunate and inaccurate form of party-line criticism on Brett Ashley, however, is that which glibly labels her a "bitch." This assessment apparently began with Edmund Wilson and his interpretation of Brett Ashley as "an exclusively destructive force," and has been perpetuated almost uniformly by critics [since the 1940s], including such notables as Philip Young, Joseph Warren Beach, Leslie Fiedler, and John Aldridge, who describes her as a "compulsive bitch." Almost to a person, the critics of the Brett-the-bitch school rely on Brett's own pronouncements for their interpretation, particularly the assertion that Brett makes to Jake after she leaves Romero: "You know it makes one feel rather good deciding not to be a bitch." This is, in fact, the single most quoted passage in criticism of the novel.

Superficially, Brett's behavior might be construed as "bitch-like." She does pursue courses of action which run counter to the wishes of the men with whom she is associated. In the early scene in the cafe, when Cohn, just introduced to Brett, fawningly asks her to dance, she lies, "I've promised to dance this with Jacob." Later, Jake and Brett discuss Brett's fiance, Mike Campbell, and Brett says, "Funny. I haven't thought about him for a week"; when Jake asks if she has written to Mike, Brett replies, "Not I. Never write letters." When Brett insists that Mike tell the story of the questionable way he received his war medals, Mike says

HEMINGWAY'S ORIGINAL "BRETT ASHLEY" OPENING

F. Scott Fitzgerald dissuaded Hemingway from using his first chapter to describe the life history of Brett Ashley. The tone in the original is dramatically more "writerly" than the "Robert Cohn" section that he eventually settled on to introduce Brett.

This is a novel about a lady. Her name is Lady Ashley and when the story begins she is living in Paris and it is Spring. That should be a good setting for a romantic but highly moral story. As every one knows, Paris is a very romantic place. Spring in Paris is a very happy and romantic time. Autumn in Paris, although very beautiful, might give a note of sadness or melancholy that we shall try to keep out of this story.

Lady Ashley was born Elizabeth Brett Murray. Her title came from her second husband. She had divorced one husband for something or other, mutual consent; not until after he had put one of those notices in the papers stating that after this date he would not be responsible for any debt, etc. He was a Scotchman and found Brett much too expensive, especially as she had only married him to get rid of him and to get away from home. At present she had a legal separation from her second husband, who had the title, because he was a dipsomaniac, he having learned it in the North Sea commanding a minesweeper, Brett said. When he had gotten to be a proper thoroughgoing dipsomaniac and found that Brett did not love him he tried to kill her, and between times slept on the floor and was never sober and had great spells of crying. Brett always declared that it had been one of the really great mistakes of her life to have married a sailor. She should have known better, she said, but she had sent the one man she had wanted to marry off to Mesopotamia so he would last out the war, and

to Cohn, "Brett will tell you. She tells all the stories that reflect discredit on me." Recall, in addition, Cohn's label of
Circe for Brett ("she turns men into swine") and, most important, the way Brett torments Jake by repeatedly not appearing for dates and by repeatedly describing her affairs
with other men, and one can see how she, and the critics following her lead, might think of herself as a bitch.

I would strongly assert that such a charge, however, is not
valid, and for three major reasons: 1. Brett and the other
characters in the novel live in a milieu in which relationships and responsibilities are intentionally loose and disor-

---

he had died of some very unromantic form of dysentery and
she certainly could not marry Jake Barnes, so when she had to
marry she had married Lord Robert Ashley, who proceeded to
become a dipsomaniac as before stated.

They had a son and Ashley would not divorce, and would
not give grounds for divorce, but there was a separation and
Brett went off with Mike Campbell to the Continent one afternoon, she having offered to at lunch because Mike was lonely
and sick and very companionable, and, as she said, "obviously
one of us." They arranged the whole business before the
Folkestone-Boulogne train left London at 9:30 that night. Brett
was always very proud of that. The speed with which they got
passports and raised funds. They came to Paris on their way to
the Riviera, and stayed the night in a hotel which had only one
room free and that with a double bed. "We'd no idea of anything of that sort," Brett said. "Mike said we should go on and
look up another hotel, but I said no, to stop where we were.
What's the odds." That was how they happened to be living
together.

Mike at that time was ill. It was all he had brought back
with him from the two years he had spent in business in
Spain, after he had left the army, except the beautifully en-
graved shares of the company which had absorbed all of the
fifteen thousand pounds that had come to him from his father's estate. He was also an undischarged bankrupt, which is
quite a serious thing in England, and had various habits that
Brett felt sorry for, did not think a man should have, and cured
by constant watchfulness and the exercise of her then very
strong will.

Frederic Joseph Svoboda, *Hemingway and* The Sun Also Rises: *The Crafting of a
Style.* Lawrence: University Press of Kansas, 1983.

dered, and her behavior merely reflects this milieu; 2. While Brett's behavior toward men is sometimes thoughtless, it is never cruel; and—central to an understanding of Brett's character—3. she is a woman who . . . has a mind disordered by the impact of the war. . . . She cannot find the route to psychological health with the result that she consistently pursues a course of self-abuse, indeed of self-destruction. . . .

EYES OF THE BEHOLDERS

Before judging Brett a bitch, then, one must measure both the milieu she is part of and—some of the time it means the same thing—the individuals whose interests she frustrates.

We turn now to the men with whom Brett is associated and the ways in which she denies their wishes. There is Robert Cohn, with whom she eventually agrees to have a brief affair. Cohn is, as Hemingway obviously intends him to be, the complete ass. He fawns over Brett; he follows her almost everywhere; he says all the wrong things; and he is a bully. Though Brett, in order to talk to Jake alone, says to Cohn, "For God's sake, go off somewhere. Can't you see Jake and I want to talk?" her outburst is probably considerably less than Cohn deserves. Far from being cruel to Cohn, on several occasions she intervenes to prevent Mike from being cruel—saying to Mike's malicious goading of Cohn, "Shut up, Michael. Try and show a little breeding." Because of his cruel, drunken tongue, Mike Campbell, like Cohn, deserves whatever thoughtlessness Brett directs his way.

The matter of Brett's relationship with Jake and whether she is cruel to him must be taken up in the larger context of Brett's attitude toward herself and the self-destructive behavior which grows out of that attitude. Critics have almost uniformly taken Brett's "deciding-not-to-be-a-bitch" statement at face value and accepted her assumption that she has, therefore, been a bitch all along. When critics like Edmund Wilson claim that Brett is "an exclusively destructive force," they are reinforcing Brett's interpretation of herself— and it is a wrong interpretation. Brett hurts no one in the novel nearly as severely as she hurts herself. Her nymphomania, her alcoholism, her constant fits of depression, and her obsession with bathing are all symptoms of an individual engaged in a consistent pattern of self-abuse. Even in causing discomfort to Jake—much of which he sets himself up for—Brett causes even greater discomfort to herself. Before one too easily accepts Robert Cohn's view of Brett as the emasculating Circe, as critic Sheridan Baker and others do, one must realize that Jake was not technically emasculated (as Hemingway made clear), and that the injury the war (a male-mission enterprise) caused Jake is far more permanent and devastating than anything that Brett does to him.

BRETT'S GOTTA HAVE IT

The most significant symptom of Brett's pursuit of self-destruction is her nymphomania. Two of the basic interpretations of nymphomania are 1. that it is merely the open expression of the "natural" female sexual appetite of insatiation which, because of centuries of social restrictions (produced by male sexual limitations), is suppressed in most women; and 2.—the more commonly held of the two—that it represents a woman's attempt to overcome social or sexual self-doubt, by demonstrating, through one sexual experience after another, that she is, in fact, attractive, desirable, wanted. By the first interpretation, Brett's milieu could be said to allow freedom from most conventions, including those of female sexual suppression, but I am convinced it is the second of the interpretations of nymphomania which more aptly applies in Brett's case. Her unsuccessful marriages, her engagement to a man she has no serious regard for, her inability to commit herself to anything meaningful—indeed her inability even to define what is meaningful—denote a mental confusion in Brett, on the matter of her own worth, which is compounded by her chronic cycle of drinking-drunkenness-recovery. Another, overlapping, cycle taints Brett's mind as well: alcohol-sex-guilt. Despite the ostensible isolation of Brett and her group from the mores of the world at large, not even Brett can completely dismiss the attitudes (in this case, regarding female drinking and sexuality) of the prevailing culture which surrounds a subculture group.

Brett's mind is, then, seriously disordered and filled with guilt. But how does this condition reflect on Brett's relationship with Jake? Quite directly actually. As psychiatrist Eric Berne points out, guilty people feel a compulsion to provide themselves with punishment; they almost always "set the stage" of their lives so as to insure themselves of painful events, thus constantly providing themselves with the punishment that their mental states require. Jake's physical condition provides precisely the kind of constant pain which

Brett needs. When critics like Sheldon Grebstein claim that Brett is the "most dramatic example . . . of how pure sex can waste lives," they overlook the rather obvious fact that Brett's sexual activity reflects not her threshold of lust but rather her threshold of self-abasement. Jake is the perfect vehicle. She can (with his encouragement) sexually tease him and herself. Midway through the arousal stage, she can step back melodramatically, acknowledge the impossibility of it all, and torment herself for initiating the action in the first place.

Such scenes of torment between Jake and Brett are common in the novel and much of the time they have the mock-seriousness of the soap opera. Near the opening, in the taxi, they kiss; then "she turned away and pressed against the corner of the seat, as far away as she could get." She says, "Don't touch me. . . . Please don't touch me." Later in the hotel, Jake asks, "Couldn't we just live together?" and Brett replies, "I'd just *tromper* you with everybody. You couldn't stand it." Still later in the cafe Brett tells Jake: "I'm so miserable," and then goes on to insure herself of a continued feeling of misery by telling Jake, "Good night, darling. I won't see you again." Even the book's conclusion reflects the tease-withdraw-suffer syndrome that has become a routine part of Brett's relationship with Jake. In a tone of agony befitting television "daytime drama," Brett says, "Oh, Jake . . . we could have had such a damned good time together."

In Brett's relationship with Romero, we see two aspects of Brett's character that demonstrate that she is a self-induced "sufferer" but that she is *not* a bitch. Early on she reminds herself, "That Romero lad is just a child," but adds, "And God, what looks." She ups the ante on her guilt not long afterward when she tells Jake (guilt coming from both directions this way), "I'm a goner. I'm mad about the Romero boy. I'm in love with him, I think," and follows immediately with the guilt payoff when she says, "I've never felt such a bitch." Brett is better than she wants to think herself, however, for this time she would not be causing discomfort to someone who deserves it (like Cohn and Mike Campbell) or to someone who consistently asks for it (like Jake). To hurt Romero would be a bitch-like act and she cannot do it. Despite what she thinks, it is simply not her style. Brett is confused; she feels guilty (hence the obsession with bathing); she is tragically self-destructive; but in no legitimate way can she be interpreted as a bitch.

The Primitive Emotion That Drives Jake Barnes

Ernest Lockridge

In this incendiary selection, Ernest Lockridge blasts both Jake and Brett as manipulative connivers who deserve to be punished. Lockridge argues that other critics who claim that Jake's "selling" of Romero to Brett is an act of love have missed the point. It is Jake's hatred for Robert Cohn—for being a Jew—that is responsible. Jake is acting out of revenge, even at his own expense. This is illustrated by the contempt he shows for Cohn; Jake considers Brett's other conquests just loveblind victims like himself. Ernest Lockridge is professor emeritus of Ohio State University and the author and editor of numerous essays and novels, including *Hatspring Blows His Mind* and *Prince Elmo's Fire.*

When Jake Barnes, narrator of Ernest Hemingway's *The Sun Also Rises*, takes his beloved Lady Ashley to "find" Pedro Romero, Barnes perpetrates the novel's central action. Its consequences are disastrous both for himself and for "ROBERT COHN," the Jew whose name supplies the first two words of the narrative and whose presence so stalks it that Barnes's story can be read as a palimpsest upon Cohn's. In addition to whatever one suffers for delivering one's love-object to someone else for servicing, the act causes Barnes to lose Montoya's friendship and, presumably, the hotel-keeper's favored treatment during any future fiestas. The deeper implication is, of course, that Montoya has excommunicated Barnes from *aficion,* the passion which unites the quasi-religious brotherhood of bullfight-worshippers who meet annually in Montoya's secular monastery, and which provides Barnes spiritual sustenance year-round,

Excerpted from "'Primitive Emotions': A Tragedy of Revenge Called *The Sun Also Rises,*" by Ernest Lockridge, *The Journal of Narrative Technique,* vol. 21, no. 1 (Winter 1990). Reprinted with permission.

compensating a bit for his war-induced impotence. Excommunication is Barnes's penalty for exposing Romero, bullfighter-saint and savior of bullfighting, to corruption and abuse by the foulest of Barnes's friends. No more brotherly laying on of hands for Barnes, or embarrassed catechisms regarding the bullfight, or all-forgiving grace provided those blessed with *aficion.*

Nor is this penalty the mere outward loss of a hotel-keeper's favor. Barnes has paid with the inner spiritual loss of *aficion.* What remains to him, aside from a little fishing with the boys, is an impotent, soul-corroding passion, persisting like addiction or chronic disease, for a jaunty, alcoholic nymphomaniac. "You gave up something," notes poor old Barnes, "and got something else." Cohn is quite simply "ruined" by Barnes's act. "I felt so terribly," Cohn informs Barnes, following the violently jealous Cohn's bash-up of Romero. "I've been through such hell, Jake," continues Cohn. "Now everything's gone. Everything." "Well," responds Barnes, "I've got to go." In the final chapter, a self-congratulatory Brett Ashley tells Barnes, "I'm all right again. [Romero's] wiped out that damned Cohn." "Good," says Barnes.

Why Barnes performs his service for Lady Ashley, performs it virtually in public, in the face of Montoya's warning and entirely predictable censure, and at such cost to himself, poses a dilemma. Barnes's motivation is perhaps the central *dramatic* problem in the novel, and here—as virtually everywhere else in discussions of *The Sun Also Rises*—criticism tends to take Barnes at his word, at his own judgment and self-explanation. As the most widely-reprinted essay on the novel tells us, Barnes, like Cohn, does what he does out of LOVE:

> . . . Brett [has] reduced [Barnes] to a slavish pimp. When she asks for his help in her affair with Pedro, Barnes . . . can only serve her as Cohn has served her, like a sick romantic steer. *Thus, for love's sake,* he will allow her to use him as a go-between, to disgrace him with his friend, Montoya, to corrupt Romero. . . . (emphasis mine)

It should be noted that Cohn's own romantic service adopts a less generous and selfless form: Cohn acts out of sexual jealousy, for revenge.

Barnes, himself, is a bit tight-lipped in elucidating his own motive, but he makes the critic's point well enough. One need only skip backward two chapters, from Chapter

XVI, in which Barnes performs his act of "love," to Chapter XIV, where he has prepared the reader for this act by elucidating his "philosophy" of "exchange of values":

> Women made such swell friends. Awfully swell. In the first place, you had to be in love with a woman to have a basis of friendship. I had been having Brett for a friend. I had not been thinking about her side of it. I had been getting something for nothing. That only delayed the presentation of the bill. The bill always came. That was one of the swell things you could count on.

> I thought I had paid for everything. Not like the woman pays and pays and pays. No idea of retribution or punishment. Just exchange of values. You gave up something and got something else.

In Chapter XVI, then, comes Lady Ashley's "presentation of the bill":

> "Do you still love me, Jake?"

> "Yes," I said.

> "Because I'm a goner. . . . I'm mad about the Romero boy. I'm in love with him, I think. . . . What do you think it's meant to have that damned Jew about. . . ."

> "What do you want me to do?"

> "Come on," Brett said. "Let's go and find him."

Whereupon Barnes proceeds to honor his "love" debt.

Q.E.D.—unless one chooses not to swallow whole Barnes's account of his own motives. What can it be that Barnes truly believes he has been "getting . . . for nothing" from Lady Ashley, besides a sadistically flaunted run of betrayals? He is by no means blind to Lady Ashley's ongoing faithlessness (cf. "This was the Brett that I had felt like crying about"). She rubs his face in it. When he does manage somehow to miss an Ashleyan trick, she patiently sets him straight: "Who did you think I went down to San Sebastian with?" What "the woman" in Barnes's specific case has been paying out is a bounty in pain and grief—nothing for something. His reasoning is disingenuously at odds with obvious reality. Moreover, the ruin of Cohn, of whose escapade with Lady Ashley Barnes confesses that he is "blind, unforgivingly jealous," would according to this reading seem to occur merely as fortuitous byproduct, an unintended result of Barnes nobly honoring his debt by using some young guy for currency, and not as an end that Barnes deliberately pursues with calculation and design.

HEMINGWAY'S MACK TRUCK

Nor does the Barnes version square with Hemingway's tech-
niques of indirection and irony in his landmark works,
which as a result demand "a considerable effort" from the
reader. "I know," Hemingway writes Owen Wister (c. 25 July
1929), "how damned much I try always to do the thing by
three cushion shots rather than by . . . direct statement." Of
course, it might be said that in *The Sun Also Rises* he took an
easy shot, one which, more than anywhere else in his early
and best work, makes him target to the charge of sentimentality, and sentimentality of a particularly trite and sappy
stamp, beneath a "tough" exterior. In the terms of Hemingway's famous metaphor describing his artistic method—"the
dignity of movement of an ice-berg is due to only one-eighth
of its being above water"—eight-eighths would here seem to
be floating about on the surface.

But in fact, Barnes's "intimate revelations," to expropriate
the self-damning formulation of F. Scott Fitzgerald's narrator
Nick Carraway, "are marred by obvious suppressions"—or,
rather, by one great big suppression that lies at the novel's
core, driving both the story and how Barnes tells it. Couched
in denial and self-disgust, Barnes's suppressed motive leaks,
here, from around the periphery of his "fine philosophy":
"The bill always came. . . . No idea of retribution or punishment. Just exchange of values. . . . I liked to see [Mike] hurt
Cohn. I wished he would not do it, though, because afterward
it made me disgusted at myself." Hemingway allows Barnes
to let down his guard only once, in a "direct statement" that
comprises Barnes's one moment of complete candor:

> Why I felt that impulse to devil [Cohn] I do not know. Of
> course I do know. I was blind, unforgivingly jealous of what
> had happened to him. The fact that I took it as a matter of
> course did not alter that any. I certainly did hate him.

"[R]etribution and punishment" are by no means periph-
eral, or an eccentric singularity; they are the whole narrative's
primary mover. I will argue that the violent sexual jealousy
that Barnes bears toward Robert Cohn, and Barnes's consequent desire for revenge, motivate the novel's central action
and overall structure, from Barnes's sarcastic no-win attack
on Cohn which begins the novel, to Barnes's act of "damned
pimp[ing]," which predictably destroys Cohn, to the emotional emptiness and self-revulsion with which this Pyrrhic
victory leaves Barnes at novel's end. That the narrative-

driving force of sexual jealousy and revenge has apparently eluded the conscious awareness of critics, at least in the voluminous published criticism, is tantamount to Hemingway's having driven unnoticed through the middle of a vigilant crowd a brilliantly camouflaged Mack truck.

BARNES THROWS COHN OFF THE SCENT

The omnipresent Cohn does not function merely as some sort of thematic or allegorical "double" to Barnes. As the quarry of Barnes's jealous obsession, he is, in terms of plot, the novel's sine qua non. . . . "Why don't you start living your life in Paris?" an exasperated Barnes asks Cohn in Chapter II, when Cohn is entertaining thoughts of going to South America. The way in which Cohn begins following this advice in Chapter III must seem to Barnes a pleasant irony: "I saw Robert Cohn looking at [Brett] a great deal as his compatriot must have looked when he saw the promised land." "You've made a new one there," Barnes tells Lady Ashley. Barnes does not find out until after her return from San Sebastian what her extended conversation with Cohn portends ("Cohn was talking to her. . . . Cohn was still talking to Brett"), but the Barnes who is narrating all this in retrospect knows only too well—just as he knows that Cohn's reason subsequently for remaining in Paris is *not* Frances Clyne, it is Brett Ashley.

That Barnes apprehends Cohn as a rival underlies their brilliantly written skirmish in Chapter V, after Cohn's first encounter with Lady Ashley. "Thought any more about going to South America?" Barnes asks Cohn. "Well, why don't you start off?" Barnes pursues, though it is now entirely too late. When Cohn confides, "I shouldn't wonder if I were in love with [Brett]," the tone and substance of Barnes's response reveal something quite other than merely "trying to give [Cohn] the facts": "She's a drunk," asserts Barnes. "She's in love with Mike Campbell, and she's going to marry him. He's going to be rich as hell some day. . . . She's thirty-four. . . . She's [married somebody she didn't love] twice." By blackening Lady Ashley's character, a suspicious and jealous Barnes attempts to put off Cohn from pursuing her. When, near the end of this exchange, Cohn tells Barnes, "You're really the best friend I have, Jake," Barnes thinks, "God help you. . . ."

After Lady Ashley informs Barnes, in Chapter IX, of her affair with Cohn, Barnes's narrative bristles with assaults, large and small, on Cohn: from sarcasm in the narrative voice, to deviling Cohn and helping to scapegoat him, to an ultimate devilment which undoes Cohn completely. Following Lady Ashley's confidence almost everything Cohn says and does, no matter how innocent or innocuous it might seem in any other context, is somehow wrong. Beneath Barnes's tone lies an omnipresent sneer: "Cohn made some remark about [the cathedral] being a very good example of something or other, I forget what. It seemed like a nice cathedral . . ."; "[w]e paid for the beers, we matched and I think Cohn paid"; "Robert Cohn asked, pointing with his finger, if there were any trout in the stream . . ."; "I was up in front with the driver and I turned around. Robert Cohn was asleep, but Bill looked and nodded his head"; "[Cohn] said it with an air of superior knowledge that irritated both of us"; "Robert Cohn had taken a bath, had had a shave and a haircut and a shampoo, and something put on his hair afterward to make it stay down"—to which Barnes adds, "He was nervous, and I did not try to help him any." These sneering nuances are underscored when Barnes says, "I do not think I ever really hated him until he had that little spell of superiority at lunch—that and when he went through all that barbering."

Barnes makes Cohn a target of "devilment" immediately following Lady Ashley's little confidence in Chapter IX, when, knowing that her presence in Spain will be "rough on [Cohn]," Barnes directs her to "Tell him you're coming." At the end of Chapter IX, Cohn appears and Barnes introduces Bill Gorton to him as "Bill Grundy." This seemingly pointless mistake is actually a petty tactic to throw Cohn off balance, though in spite of nearsightedness, Cohn manages "to make . . . out" Gorton's true identity and to say something nice. In the next chapter, X, Barnes continues to "devil" Cohn and to enjoy it:

> Cohn got up from the table and said he would go to the station [to see if Brett had arrived]. I said I would go with him, just to devil him. . . . I was enjoying Cohn's nervousness. I hoped Brett would be on the train. . . . I have never seen a man in civil life as nervous as Robert Cohn. . . . I was enjoying it. It was lousy to enjoy it, but I felt lousy.

Barnes pockets Lady Ashley's telegram, though "ordinarily [he] should have handed it over" to Cohn, and falsifies its content. It is then that Barnes admits that his "impulse to devil" Cohn derives from blind, unforgiving jealousy, which lends another passage near the beginning of Chapter X an unmistakable ominousness in its juxtaposition of Cohn and a cockroach:

> While we were waiting [for Robert Cohn] I saw a cockroach on the parquet floor that must have been at least three inches long. I pointed *him* out to Bill and then put my shoe on him. . . .
>
> Cohn came down finally. . . . (emphasis mine)

Barnes wants to crush Cohn. He requires only opportunity and means, and these present themselves in the shapely form of Pedro Romero.

Fuchs claims that Barnes "does what he can to keep Romero from" Lady Ashley, but precisely the opposite is true. Barnes observes, on first seeing Romero, "He was the best-looking boy I have ever seen"; when Montoya asks if Barnes doesn't think Romero is a "fine boy," Barnes returns to Romero's looks: "'He's a good-looking kid,' I said." Predictably, Lady Ashley agrees: "'Oh, isn't he lovely,' Brett said. 'And those green trousers.'" "Brett never took her eyes off them," Mike informs Barnes. Then comes this exchange:

> "I want to sit down below, next time." Brett drank from her glass of absinthe.
>
> "She wants to see the bull-fighters close by," Mike said.
>
> "They are something," Brett said. "That Romero lad is just a child."
>
> "*He's a damned good-looking boy*," I said. "When we were up in his room *I never saw a better-looking kid.*"
>
> "*How old do you suppose he is?*"
>
> "Nineteen *or twenty.*"
>
> "Just imagine it." (emphasis mine)

Here, responding to Lady Ashley's "just a child" comment, Barnes twice emphasizes Romero's physical attractiveness and—having learned shortly before that "[the] boy was nineteen years old"—exaggerates the bullfighter's age. These are not the remarks of a man who wants to keep a woman at arm's length from another man. On the contrary, Barnes is enticing Lady Ashley with Romero's extraordinary looks. He is suggesting that what she doubtless imagines is not cradle-robbing. Most significantly, Barnes has begun hinting to Lady Ashley not only that he knows whither her appetites are tending but that he is in complete sympathy. He approves.

THE BULLFIGHT

The following day at the bullfight, Barnes extolls to Lady Ashley, a rapid learner, the extraordinary virtues of Romero's technique: "I sat beside Brett and explained to Brett what it was all about. . . . I had her watch how Romero took the bull . . . smoothly and suavely. . . ." Under Barnes's tutelage, she sees "how Romero [avoids] every brusque movement . . . how close Romero always [works] to the bull . . . why she [likes] Romero's capework," etc. Barnes's bullfight-appreciation lesson ends with this exchange among Barnes, Lady Ashley, and Mike:

"And God, what looks," Brett said.

"I believe, you know, that she's falling in love with this bull-fighter chap," Mike said.

"I wouldn't be surprised."

"Be a good chap, Jake. Don't tell her anything more about him. Tell her how they beat their old mothers."

"Tell me what drunks they are."

"Oh, frightful," Mike said. "Drunk all day and spend all their time beating their poor old mothers."

"He looks that way," Brett said.

"Doesn't he?" I said. (emphasis mine)

Mike's nervous banter reveals his distinct unease regarding Barnes's selling of Romero to Lady Ashley. An enlarged appreciation of Romero's bullfighting has certainly not blinded Mike's fiancée to Romero's "looks." Barnes, meanwhile, subtly encourages Lady Ashley to believe that her desire for Romero is fine, even rather ennobling, and that Barnes is on her side. As Barnes has said of the bullfight, "something [is] going on with a definite end."

Barnes's secret agenda, to bring Lady Ashley and Romero together, achieves results the next day. Lady Ashley proposes to Barnes, "'You might introduce your friends. . . .' She had not stopped looking at Pedro Romero." Right after Barnes performs the introductions, Romero takes the bait, "sitting beside Brett and listening to her," "fingering his glass and talking with Brett. Brett was talking French and he was talking Spanish and a little English, and laughing." Mike's jabbing at Cohn, already a source of *Schadenfreude* for Barnes, gains in intensity, because Mike now displaces his newly aroused jealousy of Romero onto Cohn. Mike progresses from, "Tell

[Romero] Brett wants to see him put on those green pants," to, "Do you think you amount to something, Cohn? Do you think you belong here among us? . . . Do you think Brett wants you here. . . . Go away. . . . Take that sad Jewish face away." Cohn, whose presence Barnes omits to mention for more than three pages into the scene, is witness to everything, including Barnes's introduction and Lady Ashley's exclamatory outrageousness: "My God! he's a lovely boy. . . . And how I would love to see him get into those clothes. He must use a shoe-horn." Cohn's own inevitable jealousy of Romero—of the matador's youth, vitality, skill, beauty, and prominent virility—coupled with Mike's persistent attacks, goads Cohn into readiness "to do battle for his lady love." So effectively have Barnes's manipulations worked that events now have their own momentum.

Montoya walks in on this spectacle and catches Barnes at his dirty work:

> [Montoya] started to smile at me, then he saw Pedro Romero with a big glass of cognac in his hand, sitting laughing between me and a woman with bare shoulders, at a table full of drunks. He did not even nod.

At this moment Barnes must feel that he irrevocably loses Montoya's respect. Further, through the disapproving eyes of an outsider whom he deeply respects, Barnes can see more clearly the dismal effect his actions are having upon people he has no desire to harm: these are not the "friends" he wants to "kill." But he will do nothing to arrest the momentum; his hatred for Cohn is simply too profound. Thus when Mike begins a toast "to—," Barnes butts in with "Pedro Romero," in sardonic recognition that, his instrument of revenge in place, Barnes himself has stepped over the precipice.

COHN GETS THE BILL

Events begin unravelling with the predictability of "some bad play." Lady Ashley tests the water to make certain she still has the power to get what she wants out of Barnes: "Do you still love me, Jake?" His "Yes" precipitates the self-pity he has heard so often before—most notably at the end of Book I, where she says, "Oh, darling . . . I'm so miserable," and Barnes has "that feeling of going through something that has all happened before . . . as in a nightmare of it all being something repeated, something I had been through and that now

I must go through again." Vocal self-pity is Lady Ashley's tried-and-true method of twisting Barnes's reins. Now, after announcing, "I'm mad about the Romero boy," she commences with: "I've never been able to help anything. . . . I've lost my self-respect. . . . What do you think it's meant to have that damned Jew about," etc. Finally Barnes has heard enough. "What do you want me to do?" he asks—as if he didn't know. Lady Ashley drops her routine and comes to the point: "Come on. . . . Let's go and find him." Barnes may have little appetite for what he is about to accomplish, but he will not be sidetracked; when she says of Romero, "I can't look at him," Barnes, pandering away, counters with, "He's nice to look at." Romero, who has already displayed plenty of interest in Lady Ashley, is as predictable as any other healthy heterosexual male teenager. Cohn, the object of Barnes's jealous hatred and covert manipulation, is ruined by his own jealous hatred of Romero. In terms of the Barnes "philosophy," Cohn has "been getting something for nothing. That only delayed the presentation of the bill. The bill always came." Barnes has now seen to it that Cohn receives "retribution and punishment," that he "pays and pays and pays."

COHN'S INNOCENCE

Nowhere in *The Sun Also Rises* is there any indication that Cohn knows anything at all of Barnes's impotence or of his love for Lady Ashley. Thus Cohn cannot be accused of cruelty toward Barnes, or even of conscious rivalry; at worst, Cohn is somewhat unobservant. Bill Gorton knows of Barnes's wound, presumably because Barnes has confided in him, something Barnes has never done and would never do with Cohn. Yet even Gorton must figure out on his own Barnes's feelings for Lady Ashley, a task which Barnes tries to confound by feigning disinterest, for example saying to Gorton at one point, "Mike was pretty excited about his girl friend." Barnes, who would "a hell of a lot rather not talk about it," has obviously not talked about it to Cohn, who is less observant than Gorton and as a result gets blind-sided. Cohn sees his "best friend," his "only friend," inexplicably pimping the woman Cohn "[loves] so" to another man—and that is all he sees. Nevertheless, Cohn begs Barnes's forgiveness and from the depths of his misery is able to express concern for his nemesis. His exit line is: "Are you all right, Jake?" Cohn never knows what, or who, hits him and is destroyed from behind—"[a] big horn wound right through the back"—in the dark, by an enemy he cannot see.

During their final scene together, Barnes notes that "[i]n the dark I could not see [Cohn's] face very well." There are similar moments—"Somehow I feel I have not shown Robert Cohn clearly"; "[he] was a little nearsighted. I had never noticed it before"—which hint of Barnes's own blindness to Cohn. "[B]lind, unforgivingly jealous," Barnes has become virtually blind to Cohn's membership in the human race, which leads to Barnes's placing blinders on the reader. Beginning with the patronizing sarcasm of the opening sentences, Barnes's narrative strategy is to excommunicate Robert Cohn from all human sympathy:

> ROBERT COHN was once middleweight boxing champion of Princeton. Do not think that I am very much impressed by that as a boxing title, but it meant a lot to Cohn. He cared nothing for boxing. . . . I never met any one of his class who remembered him. They did not even remember that he was middleweight boxing champion.

Cohn's very honesty and niceness, impossible to deny, become liabilities: "I mistrust all frank and simple people, especially when their stories hold together," etc. The first chapter's devastation far exceeds Cohn's offenses of naivete and gaucheness—certainly it exceeds any quantifiable offense by Cohn against Barnes—and things are just beginning: Chapter I sends merely an invitation to the reader to participate in the drawn-out scapegoating of Robert Cohn. The very inditing of the story thus becomes an extension of the vengeance which now consumes Barnes entirely. Not content with having ruined Cohn in life, Barnes casts the account of what happened along a trajectory designed to ruin Cohn forever. History belongs, as usual, to the victor. . . .

BARNES'S MOTIVE

And what is it, really, that makes Barnes so all-consuming jealous of Cohn? "[T]he fact that" Barnes takes the affair itself "as a matter of course" does not in any way "alter" his hatred of Cohn. Barnes knows that Lady Ashley is chronically promiscuous, that she is on the verge of marrying yet another man. What could suddenly have the power to create such a quantum leap in this primitive emotion? Barnes provides an explanation of sorts, but one where the effect seems grossly out of all proportion to the cause: "I do not think I ever really hated him until he had that little spell of supe-

riority at lunch—that and when he went through all that
barbering." Bill, however, also present at Cohn's "little
spell of superiority," begins providing the true answer:
"Well, let him not get superior and Jewish." Barnes's
friends, including Lady Ashley, who refers to her latest sexual partner as "that damned Jew," are given to expressions
of anti-Semitism. But then so is Barnes:

> He was so good that Spider promptly overmatched him and
> got his nose permanently flattened. This increased Cohn's
> distaste for boxing, but it gave him a certain satisfaction of
> some strange sort, and it certainly improved his nose.

> He had a hard, Jewish, stubborn streak.

> She stood holding the glass and I saw Robert Cohn looking at
> her. He looked a great deal as his compatriot must have looked
> when he saw the promised land. Cohn, of course, was much
> younger. But he had that look of eager, deserving expectation.

> ". . . Haven't you got some more Jewish friends you could
> bring along?" [asks Bill.]

> "You've got some fine ones yourself," [says Barnes].

Criticism has attempted to explain anti-Semitism in *The Sun
Also Rises* in terms of forces external to any meaningful design within the novel: as an effect of the anti-Semitism of
Hemingway's era and of the fact that Harold Loeb, a model
for Cohn, happened to be a Jew.

I would argue, however, that anti-Semitism is artistically
central to *The Sun Also Rises*. Anti-Semitism is not a flaw in
the novel; it is the deepest flaw in the novel's *narrator,* the
flaw upon which his jealous hatred is predicated. . . . No "little spell of superiority at lunch . . . and when [Cohn] went
through all that barbering" carries sufficient power to
arouse Barnes's undying hatred and his obsession with
evening the score by arousing the same jealousy in Cohn.
Cohn may be childish and annoyingly gauche, but such
traits provide pale motive indeed for the depth of Barnes's
hatred and the destructiveness of his revenge. Plenty of other
"chaps" manage to pass Lady Ashley's muster—among
them, an elderly Greek count, a bullfighter, an alcoholic
Englishman—without arousing in Barnes feelings that begin to approach the jealous hatred he feels toward Cohn.
Lady Ashley neither loves Cohn nor even likes him; she is
unwilling to continue the affair, a one-shot adventure that
"[doesn't] mean anything" to her—thus Cohn poses Barnes
no threat as a rival for her affection. Why should Barnes

bother himself about Cohn at all? It is Mike, who often functions in the novel as proxy assailant and spokesman for Barnes, who inadvertently provides Barnes's unspoken motive: "Brett's gone off with men. *But they weren't ever Jews . . .*" (emphasis mine). What Barnes cannot tolerate is the fact that the woman he loves has been bedded *by a Jew.*

Barnes is more forthright about his homophobia than about his anti-Semitism: he openly expresses fury toward the homosexuals in whose company Lady Ashley first appears, employing an adjective he and others later trot out against Cohn: "I know . . . you should be tolerant, but I wanted to swing on one, any one, anything to shatter that *superior,* simpering composure" (emphasis mine). Though Barnes does allow his anti-Semitism to slip out occasionally, he feels it too shameful a motive for his shameful manipulations to confess it openly. Again employing Mike's words, "[it] reflects great discredit" on him and therefore must, like those manipulations, be suppressed when he recounts the story. But *only* anti-Semitism adequately accounts for the depth of Barnes's antipathy and for his self-destroying act of vengeance. Small wonder that after doing Cohn in, Barnes feels the need to wash himself. But "the water [will] not run."

Though Barnes is in the grips of jealous obsession, it is his abiding moral sense—his profound shame and self-disgust—that makes the novel what Hemingway called it, "a damn tragedy," and that conceals both the tragic act and the tragic flaw. "I liked to see [Mike] hurt Cohn. I wished he would not do it, though, because afterward it made me disgusted at myself." Given the degree of his own offense, far beyond Mike's pathetic jibes, Barnes is too ashamed of himself to admit openly what he has done and why. Thus the novel's great obliqueness and difficulty—"only one-eighth of [the ice-berg's] being above water"—grow directly from the character of its narrator.

BARNES'S TRAGIC END

That Barnes suppresses what causes him the most shame is only human nature, but his creator makes Barnes in all other ways honest: Barnes does not conceal the facts in the case, which speak for themselves. He is a basically decent man . . . who has suffered tandem catastrophes: receiving a "funny" wound and falling in love with, of all people, Lady Ashley. "Those to whom evil is done [d]o evil in return," writes Auden. It is Barnes's moral sense that brings him to "the end of the line." His "death" is not physical, as befalls the revenger-hero in the traditional revenge tragedy; it is the spiritual death, the terminal self-revulsion, of someone who has done the unpardonable and knows it—and knows, further, that he has sold his soul for nothing.

By the end of *The Sun Also Rises* Barnes is in such bad shape that even Lady Ashley finally notices something is the matter and begs him not to get drunk: "You don't have to." As usual she has been lousy company for Barnes. Repeatedly expressing a desire not to talk about her escapade with Romero—"let's not talk about it. Let's never talk about it"— she is scarcely able to talk about anything else. Barnes ups his consumption of alcohol. His responses become increasingly clipped, tinged with an underlying bitterness, as he sees the obvious truth to which love has been blinding him: Lady Ashley does not love him. She never has.

If "love" carries even a fractional part of the burden that the priest in *A Farewell to Arms* assigns it—"When you love you wish to do things for. You wish to sacrifice for. You wish to serve"—all of Lady Ashley's *behavior* toward Barnes, which he clearly and painfully recounts throughout his narrative, reveals that she does not love him: her mockery when she finds him with a prostitute ("'It's in restraint of trade,' Brett said. She laughed again"), her tormenting game of kiss-me/kiss-me-not, her casual desertion of him for Mippipopolous, her efforts at pitting Barnes and Mippipopolous against one another as rivals, her standing Barnes up, going off with Cohn and making sure Barnes knows, giving Bill the eye in Barnes's presence, being openly intimate with Mike, grossly displaying her appetite for Romero and making clear that her sole concern is for *his* physical condition when she disregards Barnes's timid bid for a moment of sympathy ("Knocked me out," Barnes tells her, regarding Cohn, "[t]hat was all." "I say," responds Lady Ashley, "he did hurt Pedro Romero, . . . hurt him most badly." Lady Ashley's one "true love" died of dysentery, and every man since has existed for his utility—as bed-partner, drinking buddy, rescuer. She likes to add them up, to let them down; their pitiable rivalries elevate her low self-esteem. But she does not love them. When she tells the clear-eyed Mippipopolous, whose arrow wounds are healed over, "I love you, count," he can see that "it isn't true."

Because Barnes loves her so slavishly, she knows that she can manipulate him into a variety of services, such as providing rescue money, a shoulder to weep on, and introductions to other men. Like the homosexuals with whom she and Barnes change partners (Chapter III), Barnes is someone she "can drink [with] in such safety, too." And, like her dalliance with Cohn, "it [doesn't] mean anything." Barnes is entirely correct to "suppose she only wanted what she couldn't have," but what she wants is her dead "true love." Thus Barnes's irony without pity when he responds to Lady Ashley's, "Oh, Jake . . . we could have had such a damned good time together": "Isn't it pretty to think so." Losing in the end even the illusion that he has been loved, the winner takes nothing.

Good Old Harris in *The Sun Also Rises*

Jane E. Wilson

Hemingway scholar Jane E. Wilson finds that Jake and Bill's fishing partner, Harris, personifies the generosity of spirit so lacking among Jake's friends. Their pastoral interlude is the only experience Jake has that can be considered positive. Whereas Jake's friends of many years are constantly sucking him dry, Harris provides perfect company, gives meaningful going-away presents, and refuses to wear out his welcome. Though Harris is as seemingly unaffected by the war as Robert Cohn, Jake does not resent him. It is after Jake leaves Harris's company that his universe begins to unravel.

Interpretive debate centers on whether the fishing trip is indicative of healthful rejuvenation or degenerative loss for Jake. The narration of the conclusion of the fishing episode, especially when the introduction of Harris is considered, adds to the case for the former. In contrast to most of the novel, which is narrated in detailed episodic segments (even to the point of elongating the time spent at the fiesta), Jake compresses the activity of the fishing trip: "We stayed five days at Burguete and had good fishing. The nights were cold and the days were hot . . . so that it felt good to wade in a cold stream, and the sun dried you when you came out and sat on the bank." This passage is "a decided exception" for a narrator "possessed of an obsessive aversion to the iterative." Although scholar Warren Wedin points to a lack of evidence of "good fishing," Jake's simplification of the trip and his delineation of its healthful, natural aspects indicates that he, at least, remembers the trip as a good one. Furthermore, the introduction of Harris at this point in the narrative emphasizes the positive aspects of the fishing expedition.

Harris is on his own trip to Burguete. From the very beginning, the trio of Jake, Bill, and Harris appears as separate and different from the other groups in the novel: "In the evenings we played three-handed bridge with an Englishman named Harris. . . . He was very pleasant and went with us twice to the Irati River. There was no word from Robert Cohn nor from Brett and Mike." This group is independent (they do not even need a fourth for a bridge game), and their interactions are never touched by the disruptive forces of Jake's other friends. Harris is associated with Jake and Bill and dissociated from Cohn, Brett, and Mike. Just as Burguete offers a tranquil rest from the settings of Paris and Pamplona, Harris offers a healthful interlude from Jake's relationships with the other characters.

The manuscript of the novel offers evidence of the development of the episode and the characters in it. Hemingway changed the duration of the fishing trip from three to four to five days in his manuscript revisions. He also condensed a conversation between Jake and Bill about their travel plans for the larger group. These revisions increase the role of the fishing trip and reduce the intrusion of outside forces. In the manuscript, Harris is referred to only as an "Englishman" until the morning he gives Jake the letter from Mike: "The Englishman, his name was Harris, was [looking] reading the paper again." In the final version of the novel, however, Harris is named when he is first mentioned. The emphasis on the trip and the immediate identification of Harris indicate that the character and the episode were being given greater importance in the final version.

THE WELCOME THIRD WHEEL

The most obvious points of association between Harris, Jake, and Bill are their shared love of fishing and their continual acknowledgment that they enjoy each other's company. Harris, like Jake, has "not had much fun since the war," and he displays a need to return to natural sport. He refuses Jake's offer to join them in Pamplona because he has "not much more time to fish." When Jake and Bill leave Burguete, Harris gives them "his card, with his address in London and his club and his business address." In the manuscript, Harris simply gives the Americans "his address in London." Like Jake and Bill (and unlike the others), Harris is not a disillusioned expatriate but a well-established professional, which seems to lend some order and responsibility to his life beyond the trip.

In actual representation, Harris most closely resembles the character of Bill. Both prefer fly-fishing to Jake's method of using worms for bait. Harris even reflects Bill's speech patterns. His observation to Jake that it is "wonderful how one loses track of the days up here in the mountains" echoes Bill's semi-serious, semi-ironic descriptions of the United States, New York, Vienna, and Budapest as "wonderful." Harris's reply of "What a pity" to the announcement of Jake and Bill's departure is a repetition of Bill's "irony and pity" refrain. Jake calls attention to Harris's imitation of Bill's speech ("He had taken up utilizing from Bill"), but he also gives an example of Bill's repeating Harris's assertion that it will "give . . . pleasure" to buy a round of drinks. This points to the flow of their conversation: "'Isn't that a pub across the way?' Harris asked. 'Or do my eyes deceive me?' 'It has the look of a pub,' Bill said. 'It looks to me like a pub,' I said. 'I say,' said Harris, 'let's utilize it.'" The conversations among Harris, Bill, and Jake have the same humorous comfort that distinguishes Jake's conversations with Bill alone. Some of the rhythm of these conversations is built around subtle changes Hemingway made to the dialogue in the manuscript. When the trio leaves the monastery at Roncesvalles, Bill's claim that "It's not the same as fishing" in the draft is changed to "it isn't . . ." in the novel. This leads to Harris's observation "Isn't that a pub. . . ." Bill's claim that "It has the look of a pub" originally read "It has every appearance of a pub"; the amended version leads into Jake's "It looks to me like a pub." Finally, as the trio is drinking in the pub in question, Harris expresses his pleasure in their company and Bill responds. In the original draft he tells Harris they have had a "damned good time," but in the novel the phrase is a "grand time." The revision is closer to Harris's own British style of conversation. In each case the repetition and imitation add to the rhythm of the dialogue and point to the harmony of the group.

An immediate kinship exists among these three men. Gerald T. Gordon claims that "to a degree, he [Harris] is an enigmatic representative of Jake and Bill if only in that he typifies the loneliness of the quest, the loneliness of attempting to survive with grace and dignity." Harris does remain alone, but that choice is not as bleak as Gordon makes it appear. Just as Jake later finds some order and peace when he retreats to San Sebastian at the end of the novel, Harris recognizes that he would be better off fishing alone on the Irati than joining the crowd at Pamplona. Gordon also asserts that a certain distance exists between Harris and his two new friends. He claims that Jake and Bill are at first "put off" by Harris but later warm to him because he passes a series of tests for "code" values. The Englishman, according to Gordon, never quite understands the American pair or reaches their level of verbal sophistication. On the contrary, as is shown in the give-and-take of conversation, Harris is accepted from the beginning by both Jake and Bill.

As Opposed To

Harris's similarities to his fishing partners align his character with wholesome, natural values; this association is strengthened in contrast to Mike Campbell, Brett Ashley, and Robert Cohn. As Jake and Bill leave Burguete, they express regret that Harris will not be joining them in Pamplona but immediately acknowledge that "you couldn't tell how English would mix with each other, anyway." The implication is, of course, that Harris is different from and would not mix with the group from Paris. When Jake and Bill tell their companions in Pamplona about Harris, a direct link is drawn between him and Mike by Bill's facetious question, "Ever know him, Mike? He was in the war, too." A comparison is drawn later in the novel, after the fiesta, when Jake, Bill, and Mike roll dice to see who will pay for drinks in the bar at Biarritz. Mike loses and confesses that he has no money; he cannot pay for the drinks or for his share of the car that the trio has rented. This contrasts with the scene in Burguete in which Harris will not allow Jake or Bill to pay for their drinks because he has enjoyed their company so much. Harris's present of fishing flies is another payment for his good time. The gift is an ironic one because Jake fishes with worms. Although Jake's method of fishing causes him to be labeled a "lazy bum" by Bill and creates a "rather unsportsmanly image," Harris shows great faith in his American friend. The gift of hand-tied flies is a precious one; by giving it, Harris openly demonstrates that he respects the values of the American pair and cherishes the time they have spent together. Like Jake and Bill, and unlike Mike, Harris displays an understanding of value and the need for payment.

One night in Pamplona, Jake lies awake and his thoughts travel from his friends' behavior while they were drunk, to morality, to speech patterns: "What rot, I could hear Brett say it. . . . The English spoken language—the upper classes, anyway—must have fewer words than the Eskimo. . . . I liked them, though. I liked the way they talked. Take Harris. Still Harris was not the upper classes." Jake then abruptly turns on the light and begins to read. This becomes a complicated connection between Brett and Harris. Jake seems to associate Brett with undeveloped communication, then tries to create approval for this lack by associating it with Harris, but this association falls through because Harris and Brett are essentially different (according to Jake, because of social class). Finally, Jake gives up and picks up his book, Turgenieff's *A Sportsman's Sketches*; he says, "I would remember it somewhere, and afterward it would seem as though it had really happened to me. I would always have it. That was another good thing you paid for and then had." This quotation reflects a desire to retreat into a healthy outdoor life and a reasonable system of payment, demonstrated earlier by Harris. Jake is beginning to realize the destructive nature of his relationship with Brett and to contrast it, in some way, with the healthy, natural, and ordered influences in his life.

Harris also displays a striking contrast to Robert Cohn, most obvious in Bill's reactions to each of them. Harris is welcomed into the fishing group and is repetitively assured that he is liked. His shortened name even becomes an indication of his acceptance: "'Good old Wilson-Harris,' Bill said. 'We call you Harris because we're so fond of you.'" On the other hand, while Bill acknowledges that he likes Cohn, he also tells Jake that Robert "makes me sick, and he can go to hell, and I'm damn glad he's staying here so we won't have him fishing with us." Communication is the most striking point of contrast between Harris and Cohn. Cohn's use of Spanish results in a "lousy" telegram: "Vengo Jueves Cohn." Jake and Bill's reaction to the telegram is immediately followed by Harris's admirable use of Spanish to convince the innkeeper not to accept any payment but his; this is further evidence that he recognizes the need to pay for what he enjoys. Finally, Cohn's refusal to go to Burguete contrasts sharply with Harris's refusal to go to Pamplona. Jake sees Cohn's fouled-up rendezvous with Brett and Mike as ridiculous and his excuses as insincere. He sarcastically mentions that Cohn is "sentimental" about not going fishing. Harris's refusal, on the other hand, is narrated as honestly regretful but understandable. He wishes Jake and Bill could stay, but he will not leave because he must do more fishing.

Harris's character remains directly aligned with Jake and Bill and opposed to Mike, Brett, and Cohn. The introduction of Harris at the close of the fishing expedition confirms that the trip is a regenerative one; he becomes representative of health to Jake. Harris espouses the same values Jake holds important, and he directly mirrors Bill, the least destructive and most healthy character in the novel. His appearance in the trip to Burguete links the trip to positive values and to health and normality, and it separates the trip from the chaotic influence of the other characters.

THE LAST GOOD DAY

On their last day in Burguete, Jake and Bill accompany Harris to the monastery of Roncesvalles. Their ability to enjoy the visit together is a sanctifying episode in their association. Jake is silent while Bill and Harris acknowledge that the monastery is "remarkable" but "not the same as fishing." The allusion to the betrayal of the hero in the epic *Chanson de Roland* and Jake's silence suggest that traditional and theological values are important to him. There is also the suggestion that he might anticipate the episodes about to unfold in Pamplona, but he quickly begins to banter with the other two about the pub. If Jake does feel foreboding, it can be quickly dismissed in this company.

This peaceful interlude cannot last forever, though. Jake leaves Burguete for the fiesta in Pamplona and enters a vastly different social situation. His relationships with Harris and Bill are based on mutual respect and liking in contrast to those in Pamplona, where each of the human relationships is tinged with irreverence and bitterness. By the end of the fiesta, Jake has forfeited nearly everything he values. He has lost control with Cohn, and he has betrayed his *afición* for bullfighting and his passion for Brett by introducing her to Romero. He has lost himself; the world "was just very clear and bright, and inclined to blur at the edges. . . . I looked strange to myself in the glass." To begin to recover, he must be alone, and he returns to a natural setting to begin the regenerative process.

In Jake's narration, the fishing expedition is the one

worthwhile experience he is able to keep. He consistently re-members it as a good time, and his relationships with his fishing companions, Harris and Bill, remain cordial and open. The relationship with Harris is one of the keys to the meaning of the fishing episode and its beneficial aspects. By introducing Harris at the end of the trip, Hemingway allows Jake, as narrator, to close the expedition with a positive force and to remember the episode as an affirmation of humane, natural values in contrast to the degeneration that follows.

CHAPTER 3

Themes in *The Sun Also Rises*

READINGS ON
THE SUN ALSO RISES

The Death of Love in *The Sun Also Rises*

Mark Spilka

Mark Spilka is a professor of English at Brown University, the editor of *Novel*, a forum on fiction, and the author of numerous articles on literature. In this seminal essay from 1958, he explores the ways in which Hemingway portrayed a "generation" of victims incapable of love for a variety of reasons, all stemming from the war. Spilka surmises that Jake, who wants to be like Romero but, because of his wound, is reduced to being more like the hapless Cohn, finally bitterly accepts the hopelessness of his situation.

> She turns and looks a moment in the glass,
> Hardly aware of her departed lover;
> Her brain allows one half-formed thought to pass:
> "Well now that's done: and I'm glad it's over."
> When lovely woman stoops to folly and
> Paces about her room again, alone,
> She smoothes her hair with automatic hand,
> And puts a record on the gramophone.

T.S. Eliot, The Waste Land

One of the most persistent themes of the twenties was the death of love in World War I. All the major writers recorded it, often in piecemeal fashion, as part of the larger postwar scene; but only Hemingway seems to have caught it whole and delivered it in lasting fictional form. His intellectual grasp of the theme might account for this. Where D.H. Lawrence settles for the shock of war on the Phallic Consciousness, or where Eliot presents assorted glimpses of sterility, Hemingway seems to design an extensive parable. Thus, in *The Sun Also Rises*, his protagonists are deliberately shaped as allegorical figures: Jake Barnes and Brett Ashley are two lovers desexed by the war; Robert Cohn is the false knight who challenges their despair; while Romero, the stalwart bullfighter, personifies the good life which will survive their failure. Of course, these characters are not abstractions in the text; they are realized through the most concrete style in American fiction, and their larger meaning is implied only by their response to immediate situations. But the implications are there, the parable is at work in every scene, and its presence lends unity and depth to the whole novel.

Barnes himself is a fine example of this technique. Cut off from love by a shell wound, he seems to suffer from an undeserved misfortune. But as most readers agree, his condition represents a peculiar form of emotional impotence. It does not involve distaste for the flesh, as with Lawrence's crippled veteran, Clifford Chatterley; instead Barnes lacks the power to control love's strength and durability. His sexual wound, the result of an unpreventable "accident" in the war, points to another realm where accidents can always happen and where Barnes is equally powerless to prevent them. In Book II of the novel he makes this same comparison while describing one of the dinners at Pamplona: "It was like certain dinners I remember from the war. There was much wine, an ignored tension, and a feeling of things coming that you could not prevent happening." This fear of emotional consequences is the key to Barnes' condition. Like so many Hemingway heroes, he has no way to handle subjective complications, and his wound is a token for this kind of impotence.

It serves the same purpose for the expatriate crowd in Paris. In some figurative manner these artists, writers, and derelicts have all been rendered impotent by the war. Thus, as Barnes presents them, they pass before us like a parade of sexual cripples, and we are able to measure them against his own forbearance in the face of a common problem. Whoever bears his sickness well is akin to Barnes; whoever adopts false postures, or willfully hurts others, falls short of his example. This is the organizing principle in Book I, this alignment of characters by their stoic qualities. But stoic or not, they are all incapable of love, and in their sober moments they seem to know it.

For this reason they feel especially upset whenever Robert Cohn appears. Cohn still upholds a romantic view of life, and since he affirms it with stubborn persistence, he acts like a goad upon his wiser contemporaries. As the narrator, Barnes must account for the challenge he presents them and the decisive turn it takes in later chapters. Accordingly, he begins the book with a review of Cohn's boxing career at Princeton. Though he has no taste for it, college boxing means a lot to Cohn. For one thing, it helps to compensate for anti-Semitic treatment from his classmates. More subtly, it turns him into an armed romantic, a man who can damage others in defense of his own beliefs. He also loves the pose of manhood which it affords him and seems strangely pleased when his nose is flattened in the ring. Soon other tokens of virility delight him, and he often confuses them with actual manliness. He likes the idea of a mistress more than he likes his actual mistress; or he likes the authority of editing and the prestige of writing, though he is a bad editor and a poor novelist. In other words, he always looks for internal strength in outward signs and sources. On leaving Princeton, he marries "on the rebound from the rotten time . . . in college." But in five years the marriage falls through, and he rebounds again to his present mistress, the forceful Frances Clyne. Then, to escape her dominance and his own disquiet, he begins to look for romance in far-off countries. As with most of his views, the source of this idea is an exotic book:

> He had been reading W.H. Hudson. That sounds like an innocent occupation, but Cohn had read and reread "The Purple Land." "The Purple Land" is a very sinister book if read too late in life. It recounts splendid imaginary amorous adventures of a perfect English gentleman in an intensely romantic land, the scenery of which is very well described. For a man to take it at thirty-four as a guidebook to what life holds is about as safe as it would be for a man of the same age to enter Wall Street direct from a French convent, equipped with a complete set of the more practical Alger books. Cohn, I believe, took every word of "The Purple Land" as literally as though it had been an R.G. Dun report.

Cohn's romanticism explains his key position in the parable. He is the last chivalric hero, the last defender of an outworn faith, and his function is to illustrate its present folly—to show us, through the absurdity of his behavior, that romantic love is dead, that one of the great guiding codes of the past no longer operates. "You're getting damned romantic," says Brett to Jake at one point in the novel. "No, bored," he replies, because for this generation boredom has become more plausible than love. As a foil to his contemporaries, Cohn helps to reveal why this is so.

Of course, there is much that is traditional in the satire on Cohn. Like the many victims of romantic literature, from Don Quixote to Tom Sawyer, he lives by what he reads and neglects reality at his own and others' peril. But Barnes and his friends have no alternative to Cohn's beliefs. There is nothing here, for example, like the neat balance between sense and sensibility in Jane Austen's world. Granted that Barnes is sensible enough, that he sees life clearly and that we are meant to contrast his private grief with Cohn's public suffering, his self-restraint with Cohn's deliberate self-exposure. Yet, emasculation aside, Barnes has no way to measure or control the state of love; and though he recognizes this with his mind and tries to act accordingly, he seems no different from Cohn in his deepest feelings. When he is alone with Brett, he wants to live with her in the country, to go with her to San Sebastian, to go up to her room, to keep her in his own room, or to keep on kissing her—though he can never really act upon such sentiments. Nor are they merely the yearnings of a tragically impotent man, for eventually they will lead Barnes to betray his own principles and to abandon self-respect, all for the sake of Lady Ashley. No, at best he is a restrained romantic, a man who carries himself well in the face of love's impossibilities, but who seems to share with Cohn a common (if hidden) weakness.

BRETT—BEAUTIFUL BUT MANNISH

The sexual parade continues through the early chapters. Besides Cohn and his possessive mistress, there is the prostitute Georgette, whom Barnes picks up one day "because of a vague sentimental idea that it would be nice to eat with some one." Barnes introduces her to his friends as his fiancée, and as his private joke affirms, the two have much in common. Georgette is sick and sterile, having reduced love to a simple monetary exchange; but like Barnes, she manages to be frank and forthright and to keep an even keel among the drifters of Paris. Together they form a pair of honest cripples, in contrast with the various pretenders whom they meet along the Left Bank. Among the latter are Cohn and Frances Clyne, the writer Braddocks and his wife, and Robert Prentiss, a rising young novelist who seems to verbalize their phoniness: "Oh, how charmingly you get angry," he tells Barnes. "I wish I had that faculty." Barnes' honest anger has been aroused by the appearance of a band of ho-

mosexuals, accompanied by Brett Ashley. When one of the
band spies Georgette, he decides to dance with her; then one
by one the rest follow suit, in deliberate parody of normal
love. Brett herself provides a key to the dizzy sexual medley.
With a man's felt hat on her boyish bob, and with her familiar reference to men as fellow "chaps," she completes the
distortion of sexual roles which seems to characterize the
period. For the war, which has unmanned Barnes and his
contemporaries, has turned Brett into the freewheeling
equal of any man. It has taken her first sweetheart's life
through dysentery and has sent her present husband home
in a dangerous state of shock. For Brett these blows are the
equivalent of Jake's emasculation; they seem to release her
from her womanly nature and expose her to the male prerogatives of drink and promiscuity. Once she claims these
rights as her own, she becomes an early but more honest
version of Catherine Barkley, the English nurse in Hemingway's next important novel, *A Farewell to Arms.* Like Catherine, Brett has been a nurse on the Italian front and has lost
a sweetheart in the war; but for her there is no saving interlude of love with a wounded patient, no rigged and timely
escape through death in childbirth. Instead she survives the
colossal violence, the disruption of her personal life, and the
exposure to mass promiscuity, to confront a moral and emotional vacuum among her postwar lovers. With this evidence
of male default all around her, she steps off the romantic
pedestal, moves freely through the bars of Paris, and stands
confidently there beside her newfound equals. Ironically,
her most recent conquest, Robert Cohn, fails to see the bearing of such changes on romantic love. He still believes that
Brett is womanly and therefore deeply serious about intimate matters. After their first meeting, he describes her as
"absolutely fine and straight" and nearly strikes Barnes for
thinking otherwise; and a bit later, after their brief affair in
the country, he remains unconvinced "that it didn't mean
anything." But when men no longer command respect, and
women replace their natural warmth with masculine freedom and mobility, there can be no serious love.

Brett does have some respect for Barnes, even a little ten-
derness, though her actions scarcely show abiding love. At
best she can affirm his worth and share his standards and
perceptions. When in public, she knows how to keep her essential misery to herself; when alone with Barnes, she will

express her feelings, admit her faults, and even display good judgment. Thus her friend, Count Mippipopolous, is introduced to Barnes as "one of us." The count qualifies by virtue of his war wounds, his invariable calmness, and his curious system of values. He appreciates good food, good wine, and a quiet place in which to enjoy them. Love also has a place in his system, but since he is "always in love," the place seems rather shaky. Like Jake and Brett and perhaps Georgette, he simply bears himself well among the postwar ruins. . . .

STRIFE IN PAMPLONA

Pamplona is an extension of Burguete for Barnes: gayer and more festive on the surface, but essentially more serious. The spoilers from Paris have arrived, but (Cohn excepted) they are soon swept up by the fiesta: their mood is jubilant, they are surrounded by dancers, and they sing, drink and shout with the peasant crowd. Barnes himself is among fellow *aficionados;* he gains "real emotion" from the bullfights and feels truly elated afterwards. Even his friends seem like "such nice people," though he begins to feel uneasy when an argument breaks out between them. The tension is created by Brett's fiancé, Mike Campbell, who is aware of her numerous infidelities and who seems to accept them with amoral tolerance. Actually he resents them, so that Cohn (the perennial Jewish scapegoat) provides him with a convenient outlet for his feelings. He begins to bait him for following Brett around like a sick steer.

Mike's description is accurate enough. Cohn is always willing to suffer in public and to absorb insults for the sake of true love. On the other hand, he is also "ready to do battle for his lady," and when the chance finally comes, he knocks his rivals down like a genuine knight-errant. With Jake and Mike he has no trouble, but when he charges into Pedro's room to rescue Brett, the results are disastrous: Brett tells him off, the bullfighter refuses to stay knocked down, and no one will shake hands with him at the end, in accord with prep-school custom. When Brett remains with Pedro, Cohn retires to his room, alone and friendless.

This last encounter is the highpoint of the parable, for in the Code Hero, the Romantic Hero has finally met his match. As the clash between them shows, there is a difference between physical and moral victory, between chivalric stubbornness and real self-respect. Thus Pedro fights to repair an affront to his dignity; though he is badly beaten, his spirit is untouched by his opponent, whereas Cohn's spirit is completely smashed. From the beginning Cohn has based his manhood on skill at boxing, or upon a woman's love, never upon internal strength; but now, when neither skill nor love supports him, he has bludgeoned his way to his own emptiness. Compare his conduct with Romero's, on the following day, as the younger man performs for Brett in the bull ring:

> Everything of which he could control the locality he did in front of her all that afternoon. Never once did he look up. . . . Because he did not look up to ask if it pleased he did it all for himself inside, and it strengthened him, and yet he did it for her, too. But he did not do it for her at any loss to himself. He gained by it all through the afternoon.

Thus, where Cohn expends and degrades himself for his beloved, Romero pays tribute without self-loss. His manhood is a thing independent of women, and for this reason he holds special attractions for Jake Barnes.

BARNES' ARRESTED DEVELOPMENT

By now it seems apparent that Cohn and Pedro are extremes for which Barnes is the unhappy medium. His resemblance to Pedro is clear enough: they share the same code, they both believe that a man's dignity depends on his own resources. His resemblance to Cohn is more subtle, but at this stage of the book it becomes grossly evident. Appropriately enough, the exposure comes through the knockout blow from Cohn, which dredges up a strange prewar experience:

> Walking across the square to the hotel everything looked new and changed. . . . I felt as I felt once coming home from an out-of-town football game. I was carrying a suitcase with my football things in it, and I walked up the street from the station in the town I had lived in all my life and it was all new. They were raking the lawns and burning leaves in the road, and I stopped for a long time and watched. It was all strange. Then I went on, and my feet seemed to be a long way off, and everything seemed to come from a long way off, and I could hear my feet walking a great distance away. I had been kicked in the head early in the game. It was like that crossing the square. It was like that going up the stairs in the hotel. Going up the stairs took a long time, and I had the feeling that I was carrying my suitcase.

Barnes seems to have regressed here to his youthful football days. As he moves on up the stairs to see Cohn, who has been asking for him, he still carries his "phantom suitcase" with him; and when he enters Cohn's room, he even sets it down. Cohn himself has just returned from the fight with Romero: "There he was, face down on the bed, crying. He had on a white polo shirt, the kind he'd worn at Princeton." In other words, Cohn has also regressed to his abject college days: they are both emotional adolescents, about the same age as the nineteen-year-old Romero, who is the only real man among them. Of course, these facts are not spelled out for us, except through the polo shirt and the phantom suitcase, which remind us (inadvertently) of one of those dreamlike fantasies by the Czech genius, Franz Kafka, in which trunks and youthful clothes are symbols of arrested development. Yet there has already been some helpful spelling out in Book I, during a curious (and otherwise pointless) exchange between Cohn and another expatriate, the drunkard Harvey Stone. After first calling Cohn a moron, Harvey asks him to say, without thinking about it, what he would rather do if he could do anything he wanted. Cohn is again urged to say what comes into his head first, and soon replies, "I think I'd rather play football again with what I know about handling myself, now." To which Harvey responds: "I misjudged you. . . . You're not a moron. You're only a case of arrested development."

A SICK ROMANTIC STEER

The first thought to enter Cohn's mind here has been suppressed by Barnes for a long time, but in Book II the knockout blow releases it: more than anything else, he too would like to "play football again," to prevent that kick to his head from happening, or that smash to the jaw from Cohn, or that sexual wound which explains either blow. For the truth about Barnes seems obvious now: he has always been an emotional adolescent. Like Nick Adams [hero of *In Our Times*], he has grown up in a society which has little use for manliness; as an expression of that society, the war has robbed him of his dignity as a man and has thus exposed him to indignities with women. We must understand here that the war, the early football game, and the fight with Cohn have this in common: they all involve ugly, senseless, or impersonal forms of violence, in which a man has little chance to set the terms of his own integrity. Hence for Hemingway they represent the kinds of degradation which can occur at any point in modern society—and the violence at

Pamplona is our current sample of such degradation. Indeed, the whole confluence of events now points to the social meaning of Jake's wound, for just as Cohn has reduced him to a dazed adolescent, so has Brett reduced him to a slavish pimp. When she asks for his help in her affair with Pedro, Barnes has no integrity to rely on; he can only serve her as Cohn has served her, like a sick romantic steer. Thus, for love's sake, he will allow her to use him as a go-between, to disgrace him with his friend, Montoya, to corrupt Romero, and so strip the whole fiesta of significance. In the next book he will even run to her rescue in Madrid, though by then he can at least recognize his folly and supply his own indictment: "That was it. Send a girl off with one man. Introduce her to another to go off with him. Now go and bring her back. And sign the wire with love. That was it all right." It seems plain, then, that Cohn and Brett have given us a

JAKE AND BRETT ARE HEALTHY

Hemingway scholar Sibbie O'Sullivan believes that Jake and Brett have a healthy, yet unconventional, bond.

If I over-emphasize that Jake's and Brett's departure from stereotypical male-female behavior is a positive dimension of their relationship, I do so because so many critics judge the couple's behavior in a negative way when measured against those stereotypes. Mark Spilka is one critic who is most ungenerous. In his essay "The Death of Love in *The Sun Also Rises*," Spilka sees Jake as emotionally impotent, as an emotional adolescent, and as a man of little integrity; according to Spilka, Jake has defaulted on his maleness. Brett fares no better. She is "the freewheeling equal of any man" who engages in the "male prerogatives of drink and promiscuity." She is a woman who allows her "natural warmth" to be replaced with "masculine freedom and mobility." Under such conditions, "there can be no serious love." Obviously Spilka identifies "serious love" with traditional male-female gender roles. Though he acknowledges the general damage to love wrought by World War I, he points specifically to the damage done when woman "steps off the romantic pedestal [and] moves freely through the bars of Paris, and stands confidently there beside her newfound equals." Such narrow-minded thinking not only oversimplifies a very complicated novel but blinds the reader to what demonstration of "serious love" there is in the book.

Sibbie O'Sullivan, *Arizona Quarterly*, Summer 1988.

peacetime demonstration, postwar style, of the meaning of Jake's shell wound.

At Pamplona the demonstration continues. Brett strolls through the fiesta with her head high, "as though [it] were being staged in her honor, and she found it pleasant and amusing." When Romero presents her with a bull's ear "cut by popular acclamation," she carries it off to her hotel, stuffs it far back in the drawer of the bed-table, and forgets about it. The ear was taken, however, from the same bull which had killed one of the crowd a few days before, during the dangerous bull-run through the streets; later the entire town attended the man's funeral, along with drinking and dancing societies from nearby communities. For the crowd, the death of this bull was a communal triumph and his ear a token of communal strength; for Brett the ear is a private trophy. In effect, she has robbed the community of its triumph, as she will now rob it of its hero. As an *aficionado,* Barnes understands this threat too well. These are decadent times in the bull ring, marred by false aesthetics; Romero alone has "the old thing," the old "purity of line through the maximum of exposure": his corruption by Brett will complete the decadence. But mainly the young fighter means something more personal to Barnes. In the bull ring he combines grace, control and sincerity with manliness; in the fight with Cohn he proves his integrity where skill is lacking. His values are exactly those of the hunter in [Hemingway's] "Francis Macomber," or of the fisherman in *The Old Man and the Sea.* As one of these few remaining images of independent manhood, he offers Barnes the comfort of vicarious redemption. Brett seems to smash this as she leaves with Pedro for Madrid. To ward off depression, Barnes can only get drunk and retire to bed; the fiesta goes on outside, but it means nothing now: the "good place" has been ruined.

"PRETTY TO THINK SO"

As Book III begins, Barnes tries to reclaim his dignity and to cleanse himself of the damage at Pamplona. He goes to San Sebastian and sits quietly there in a cafe, listening to band concerts; or he goes swimming there alone, diving deep in the green waters. Then a telegram from Brett arrives, calling him to Madrid to help her out of trouble. At once he is like Cohn again, ready to serve his lady at the expense of self-respect. Yet in Madrid he learns to accept, emotionally, what he has always faintly understood. As he listens to Brett, he begins to drink heavily, as if her story has driven home a painful lesson. Brett herself feels "rather good" about sending Pedro away: she has at least been able to avoid being "one of these bitches that ruins children." This is a moral triumph for her, as Barnes agrees; but he can scarcely ignore its implications for himself. For when Brett refuses to let her hair grow long for Pedro, it means that her role in life is fixed: she can no longer reclaim her lost womanhood; she can no longer live with a fine man without destroying him. This seems to kill the illusion which is behind Jake's suffering throughout the novel: namely, that if he hadn't been wounded, if he had somehow survived the war with his manhood intact, then he and Brett would have become true lovers. The closing lines confirm his total disillusionment:

> "Oh, Jake," Brett said, "we could have had such a damned good time together."
>
> Ahead was a mounted policeman in khaki directing traffic. He raised his baton. The car slowed suddenly pressing Brett against me.
>
> "Yes," I said. "Isn't it pretty to think so?"

"Pretty" is a romantic word which means here "foolish to consider what could *never* have happened," and not "what can't happen now." The signal for this interpretation comes from the policeman who directs traffic between Brett's speech and Barnes' reply. With his khaki clothes and his preventive baton, he stands for the war and the society which made it, for the force which stops the lovers' car, and which robs them of their normal sexual roles. As Barnes now sees, love itself is dead for their generation. Even without his wound, he would still be unmanly, and Brett unable to let her hair grow long.

Yet according to the opening epigraphs, if one generation is lost and another comes, the earth abides forever; and according to Hemingway himself, the abiding earth is the novel's hero. Perhaps he is wrong on this point, or at least misleading. There are no joyous hymns to the seasons in this novel, no celebrations of fertility and change. The scenic descriptions are accurate enough, but rather flat; there is no deep feeling in them, only fondness, for the author takes less delight in nature than in outdoor sports. He is more concerned, that is, with baiting hooks and catching trout than with the Irati River and more pleased with the grace and skill of the bullfighter than with the bull's magnificence. In fact, it is the bullfighter who seems to abide in the novel, for surely the bulls are dead like the trout before them, having fulfilled their roles as beloved opponents. But Romero is very much alive as the novel ends. When he leaves the hotel in Madrid, he "pays the bill" for his affair with Brett, which means that he has earned all its benefits. He also dominates the final conversation between the lovers, and so dominates the closing section. We learn here that his sexual initiation has been completed and his independence assured. From now on, he can work out his life alone, moving again and again through his passes in the ring, gaining strength, order, and purpose as he meets his own conditions. He provides no literal prescription to follow here, no call to bullfighting as the answer to Barnes' problems; but he does provide an image of integrity, against which Barnes and his generation are weighed and found wanting. In this sense, Pedro is the real hero of the parable, the final moral touchstone, the man whose code gives meaning to a world where love and religion are defunct, where the proofs of manhood are difficult and scarce, and where every man must learn to define his own moral conditions and then live up to them.

Alcoholism in
The Sun Also Rises

Matts Djos

Matts Djos is professor of English at Mesa State
College in Grand Junction, Colorado, and the author of extensive publications on alcohol in literature. Here he contends that without exception every
character in *The Sun Also Rises* is, by virtue of alcoholism, a manipulative self-loathing wreck incapable of genuine love or friendship. They keep their
lives deliberately disordered and permanently
doused with liquor to camouflage their spiritual
bankruptcy. The stress lines show early on, especially for the principal characters.

The Sun Also Rises is a remarkable portrait of the pathology
of the disease of alcoholism. As a description of the alcoholic
mentality, it has none of the high drama and tragic despair
of works like *Days of Wine and Roses* or *Under the Volcano*,
but this makes the story all the more realistic and compelling. Indeed, like the disease of alcoholism itself, the plot
may be quite deceptive because it presents no images of addictive self-destruction on a grandiose scale.

The novel describes how Jake Barnes and his expatriate
friends spend a good deal of time in Paris drinking and talking about drinking, how some of them make a hectic trip
over the Pyrenees to Pamplona to go fishing and watch the
bullfights, and how, after an astonishing series of affairs,
foul-ups, and misunderstandings, they straggle back to Paris
to talk some more and do some more drinking. A great deal
of the novel is focused on liquor, discussions about liquor,
hangovers, drunkenness, and finding more liquor. The following remarks are drawn from just five pages of *The Sun
Also Rises:*

"You were quite drunk my dear."

Excerpted from "Alcoholism in Ernest Hemingway's *The Sun Also Rises*: A Wine and
Roses Perspective on the Lost Generation," by Matts Djos, *Hemingway Review*, vol.14,
no. 2 (Spring 1995), pp. 64–78. Copyright © 1995 by Ernest Hemingway Foundation.
Reprinted by permission.

"I say, Jake, *do* we get a drink?"

"He loves to go for champagne."

"Let's have a drink, then. The count will be back."

"You know he's extraordinary about buying champagne. It means any amount to him."

"I think you'll find that's very good wine, . . . we don't get much of a chance to judge good wine. . . .

"This is a hell of a dull talk. . . . How about some of that champagne?"

"You're always drinking, my dear. Why don't you just talk?"

"I like to drink champagne from magnums. The wine is better but it would have been too hard to cool."

"There, my dear. Now you enjoy that slowly, and then you can get drunk."

"She is the only lady I have ever known who was as charming when she was drunk as when she was sober."

"Drink your wine."

It might be assumed that at least three of the characters—Jake Barnes, Brett Ashley, Mike Campbell—are only heavy drinkers; but there is a considerable difference between heavy drinking and the kind of self-destructive, alcoholic drinking that we read about in the novel. Indeed, Hemingway himself may have felt obliged to acknowledge the alcoholic focus of the story. When asked about its libationary focus, he appears to have grudgingly conceded that it was a "book about a few drunks"; but, as Tom Dardis notes in his excellent discussion of the writer's alcoholism, the drinking behavior described in *The Sun Also Rises* was pronounced and addictive, regardless of the motives. Hemingway may have thought that imbibing on such a monumental scale simply classified the inebriate as a sort of generic "rummy," but, as Dardis writes, he was ignorant of the fact that "alcoholism breeds its own kind of pressure, that of alcoholic depression."

Of course, in defining Mike, Brett, and Jake as practicing alcoholics, we ought to consider exactly what it is that fleshes out the portrait of someone who is alcohol-dependent; that is, we might want to consider what it is that characterizes someone whose life is dominated by an obsession with liquor.

Most social scientists have concluded that alcoholics have a higher level of anxiety, dependence, and defensiveness. This is sometimes reflected in a remarkable degree of moodiness, impulsivity, hostility, and distrust. A good number of studies have also concluded that alcoholics have lower self-esteem, are more goal-oriented, strive more for a superficial feeling of achievement, and consistently exhibit an intense need for personal power. Such problems may be manifested by the development of façades suggesting a great deal of uncertainty regarding sexual identity.

If we critique *The Sun Also Rises* with these criteria in mind, it should come as no surprise that Jake, Brett, Mike, and even Robert Cohn and Bill Gorton match the alcoholic profile in no small measure. Regardless of the setting or scene, the bars and the bottles are omnipresent and serve as a focal point for the bullfights, the eating, the peregrinating, the flirting and seducing, the fisticuffs, and even the fishing. Between Paris, Pamplona, and Burguete, Jake gets very drunk at least three times; Brett is known to get drunk twice; Mike is drunk every time we see him; Bill is rarely sober; even Cohn spends a great deal of time in his cups—and all of this happens during the two weeks or so that we as readers follow the story. Drinking on this kind of scale cannot even begin to resemble normalcy and is most certainly a substantive foundation for addiction and obsessive dependence. Of course, as with most alcoholics, any talk about abuse is usually focused on "other" people in the group, or it is jokingly discounted as the "right" kind of drinking supporting the jolly, good nature of the inner circle.

A key aspect of the alcoholic temperament is the desire for control. There is hardly a single, major character in *The Sun Also Rises* who is not a compulsive manipulator. This passion for orchestrating circumstances in conformity with certain, wilful desires is well described in *Twelve Steps and Twelve Traditions,* a major publication of Alcoholics Anonymous:

> When we habitually try to manipulate others to our own wilful desires, they [family, friends, society at large] revolt and resist us heavily. Then we develop hurt feelings, a sense of persecution, and a desire to retaliate. As we redouble our efforts at control, and continue to fail, our suffering becomes acute and constant.

Jake and his companions are terrified that fate and circumstance might shatter their façade of civilized deference. Sometimes, they barely make it from day to day; sometimes, they appear to be trying to just make it through the next hour, a common enough problem among a great many alcoholics.

These people lack the skills and the sanity to break their addiction to self-sufficiency and their destructive loop of unmanageability. Instead, they seek refuge in broken relationships, in changes of scene, in drunkenness and the illusion that, however meager, they can find some pleasure in their brief interludes of time and place. There is a great deal of fear here, fear of self-understanding, fear of emotional and physical inadequacy, and—very important—fear of each other.

THE DESCENT OF JAKE BARNES

Jake is the terminal man. Having been emasculated in the war, he has gotten tangled up in a vicious cycle of emotional self-mutilation. Regardless of whether he is alone or in company, he is resigned to the belief that he is powerless to change anything. So he secludes himself in a mantle of self-pity and hopelessness, chooses to withdraw into a Faustian tragedy of self-denial, and consigns himself to hopeless despair rather than do anything about his problem.

Jake has found a perverse kind of sainthood in the conviction that he is unique (a trait common among unrecovered alcoholics). His suffering has qualified him for a rather peculiar dementia which is likely to be manifested in bleak moods of social hatred and self-pity. Jake is something of a masochist, and his emotional starvation may well be a corollary of low self-esteem. As a consequence, he is inclined to discount his own worth and his right to any substantive fulfillment or happiness, and this may well account for his catastrophic perspective on his relationship with Brett. More often than not, he gets drunk or ends up alone in a hotel room or in his flat, staring at the ceiling while grousing about the hopelessness of his condition and the impossibility of establishing any kind of enduring connection with Brett. Thus, in his refusal to break out of his self-destructive loop, he persists in remaining self-condemned before the fact:

> My head started to work. The old grievance. Well, it was a rotten way to be wounded and flying on a joke front like the Italian. In the Italian hospital we were going to form a society. It had a funny name in Italian. . . . That was where the liaison colonel came to visit me. . . . he made that wonderful speech: "You, a foreigner, an Englishman" (any foreigner was an Englishman), "have given more than your life." What a speech! I would have like[d] to have it illuminated to hang in the office. He never laughed. He was putting himself in my place, I guess. "Che mala fortuna! Che mala fortuna!"

I never used to realize it, I guess. I try to play it along and just not make trouble for people. Probably I never would have had any trouble if I hadn't run into Brett when they shipped me to England. I suppose she only wanted what she couldn't have. Well, people were that way. To hell with people. The Catholic Church had an awfully good way of handling all that. Good advice, anyway. Not to think about it. Oh, it was swell advice. Try and take it sometime. Try and take it. I lay awake thinking and my mind jumping around. Then I couldn't keep away from it. . . . I was thinking about Brett and my mind stopped jumping. . . . Then all of a sudden I started to cry.

Like many alcoholics, Jake is convinced that his self-imposed martyrdom is terminal. He has set down the terms of his life with uncompromising severity because he is convinced that his wound is different, his front was a "joke," and he has given "more" than his life for Italy. So he feels hopeless about Brett, tries to resign himself to circumstance, and thinks about not thinking.

BRETT, MIKE, AND COHN

Like Jake, Brett is self-victimized by her catastrophic thinking and her remarkable penchant for charades and seduction. She discounts her title—Lady Brett Ashley—but seems to parade it at every opportunity. She is a voluptuary of prodigious dimensions who has learned well the game of disguising her fear of womanhood in the sexual control of men. And through it all, she canonizes herself as noble and self-sacrificing. It is a pretty little game she plays, but her strategies are riddled with drunken fakery. If viewed from a psychological-addictive perspective, Brett personifies the generic female alcoholic with a remarkable prejudice for manipulation and orchestration. She seduces; she complains; she plays the kitten; and then she runs. She targets the emotions of any man who will have anything to do with her, hopeful that he will somehow restore the integrity of her womanhood. And she knows no boundaries in her hunt. Just about anything male is fair game; any assertion of power might affirm that she is not a victim of circumstances herself. If seduction can lead to a trophy, she will seduce; if abandonment can lead to an assurance of her skill at breaking hearts, she will abandon; and if sheer, mind-boggling mental torture will do the job, then tempt and attack she will.

Mike is a masochist and village clown. He uses his money and his connections to control others, to martyr himself, and to confirm that, after all, he is little more than a drunk. If he is given a chance and enough liquor, he will attack anyone weaker than himself, a typical enough behavior of any fear-ridden alcoholic. Then, if parried too strongly, he will shake off the bully boy image and be a "good fellow." Mike has failed at just about everything—his prospects for marriage, work, sex—and he knows it and even seems rather proud of it. He adopts the pose of an idle playboy and jolly intoxicant. In truth, he is neither interested in sobering up nor skilled enough to break away from himself or his surroundings. His title and what little money he has left are sufficient to keep him mildly functional despite his drinking; his self-esteem is meager enough to keep him from even thinking about sobering up and making any real changes.

Although Cohn does not at first appear to have some of the drinking problems of his more bibulous companions, it is ironic that he provides a vivid example of some of the capricious personality flaws that are commonly perceived in the standard profile of a practicing alcoholic. Indeed, because of his insufferable emotionalism, his addiction to self-pity, and his codependent proximity to Jake's retinue, he seems to manifest the standard characteristics of a "dry drunk" or "prealcoholic" personality. Such individuals are commonly recognized around alcoholic circles because they behave like practicing alcoholics, even though they do not appear to have an addiction to or an obsessive need for liquor, as such. Indeed, they provide a striking example of the fundamental distinction between people who are "dry" and people who are "sober."

In any case, when Cohn does get drunk, he behaves like a lap dog who is trapped in insecurity and loneliness; and, like so many of his kind, finds euphoric power in illusions of masculinity. Of course, that euphoria can easily collapse in a stream of apologies and tears of self-pity, as in the drunken fight with Romero. . . .

INTIMACY IS BEYOND THEM

As far as Jake and Brett are concerned, it is assumed that genital affection is the only option in a male-female relationship; and, denied that possibility, there is no other recourse but to whine about unkind fate, refuse compromise, and dismiss the possibility that sexuality may involve a great deal more than coitus and penile fascination—as any para-

plegic would be most glad to explain. In any case, it is bla-
tantly obvious that Jake would rather withdraw into his own
misperceived loneliness, absolve himself of any opportunity
for a solution, and get drunk.

Jake's congenital preoccupation with evading any substantive consideration of his circumstances is vividly illustrated in his relationship with Bill Gorton. When Jake is
with Gorton, his closest friend, he appears to be having a
good time—indeed, the experiences and conversation seem
a long way from the standard, alcoholically dysfunctional
context of so much of the rest of the novel. However, a careful analysis of his behavior might suggest that the friendship
is severely limited—indeed, badly strained—by his fear of
personal exposure.

Certainly, when the two go fishing in the Pyrenees, the
descriptions and the scene are appealing enough. Jake and
Bill take a long walk, bait their hooks, discuss where to fish,
toss out their lines, get a nice catch, pack it, eat lunch, drink
wine, and discuss eggs and drumsticks. Later, having gotten
"cock-eyed" on wine, they have a brief conversation about
Jake's "problem":

"Say," Bill said, "what about this Brett business?"

"What about it?"

"Were you ever in love with her?"

"Sure."

"For how long?"

"Off and on for a hell of a long time."

"Oh, hell!" Bill said. "I'm sorry, fella."

"It's all right," I said. "I don't give a damn any more."

"Really?"

"Really. Only I'd a hell of a lot rather not talk about it."

And that's the end of it. Bill says he's going to sleep—and
he does.

Jake has apparently decided that intimacy must necessarily be predicated on genital voyaging. As a consequence, his
prospects for any kind of connectedness to Brett—or any-
body else for that matter—fluctuate with maddening irregu-
larity. "I've had plenty to worry about one time or other. I'm
through worrying," he says early in the novel. Even so, it
seems that he has a remarkable penchant for continuing to

worry, deny, and rationalize throughout the remainder of the story; indeed, his drunken escapades are an epic study in self-destruction, complaint, and evasion. He tells us at one point that he's gotten a "little drunk," not in any "positive sense," as he calls it, but "enough to be careless." When he's with Brett in a taxi in Paris, they kiss and discuss how his wound is "funny." "I never think about it," he lies. He burbles on to insist that he's "pretty well through with the subject," having considered it from various "angles." Of course, he feels like "hell" every time he stops being through; and, indeed, the entire novel is full of liberally sprinkled affirmations that he has quit thinking about his problem. . . .

SELF-DELUSION IS ALL THEY HAVE

Brett, Cohn, Mike, and Jake appear unaware that the true battle-ground of the self, the personal "bullring" of their fears and their wounds and their addictions, lies in how they perceive themselves and how they deal directly with their misfortunes and circumstances. Whatever enjoyments or pleasures or health they find, whatever balancing of life's risks and rewards they realize, will only be possible with an honest and fearless inventory of their own conduct, not a superficial fabrication of a code of courage and sensuality that has little to do with the business of living. However, for these alcoholics, such an inventory would be devastating. It would require a great deal more honesty than they are capable of demonstrating, and it would require too heady a dose of the very courage they claim to admire.

On the surface, then, the Hemingway "code" appears to provide a strict set of rules and values defining how the experiences of life, how courage itself, can be maximized. In this particular case, however, that "code" is degraded by the behavior of Jake, Mike, Brett, and Cohn. It promises order and meaning and resolution, but it can't deliver. The fishing scenes, the mountain idyll, and the friendships are also red herrings. Jake seeks some kind of serenity and some inner balance and wholeness when he goes fishing with Bill Gorton. But the search doesn't work—it can't work. Again, what Jake seeks has to come first from himself; it cannot be generated from a material setting or escapist impulses. In running from himself—in running to a trout stream or the mountains—he is doomed, for he can only find peace in learning to understand and accept himself for what he is.

Fish, drink, and run as he does, Jake has yet to learn to accept the fact that there is a great deal that he cannot change; and he has yet to find the courage to change what he can. So the trip is a bust. His nerves are shattered by the arrival of Cohn, by the drinking, by his loneliness and resentment, and by the pain of his wound.

The Sun Also Rises is a portrait of degeneration without solutions. It is a portrait of estrangement and emotional adolescence and "running"; and it is a portrait of a bankrupt value system that depends far too much on appearances and dramatics. It is a novel about spiritual bankruptcy, codependence, and people who enable each other to withdraw and become emotionally impotent because they support each other in erecting a meaningless façade of self-sufficiency and bathos. In the final analysis, it is a novel about people who feel compelled to fabricate a code of conduct that has very little to do with living and even less to do with their own integrity. As such, it is a portrait of what can begin to happen when emotionally damaged people seek refuge from themselves in the desensitizing and addictive effects of liquor where ignorance, insanity, escape, and waste are manifested in abundance.

Money in *The Sun Also Rises*

Patrick D. Morrow

In this excerpt from *Money Talks: Language and Lucre in American Fiction,* Patrick D. Morrow examines how Jake and his pack use money to control each other or as feeble self-defense against scrutinizing their own flawed values (i.e., Jake and Cohn). Contrary to the views of many critics, Morrow asserts that Jake is still "paying the bill" by novel's end, although his rhetoric suggests at least an awareness of his straits. Patrick D. Morrow is a professor of English at Auburn University and the author of *Bret Harte* and *Bret Harte: Literary Critic.*

> "Last week he tried to commit suicide," one waiter said.
> "Why?"
> "He was in despair."
> "About what?"
> "Nothing."
> "How do you know it was nothing?"
> "He has plenty of money."
>
>   Ernest Hemingway, "A Clean, Well-Lighted Place"

Critics have noted the importance of money in *The Sun Also Rises.* In his 1963 Twayne United States Authors Series book on Hemingway, Earl Rovit proposed that the hierarchy of the characters' financial values correlated exactly with the hierarchy of their moral values. This idea has been widely accepted. Claire Sprague in a 1969 article supports this argument, noting that in *The Sun Also Rises* "how one gets and spends money becomes a subject index to character. . . ." Sprague also asserts that Jake "chooses to believe in value, chooses to erect a rigorous personal code which his literal account-keeping parallels." Richard Sugg's 1972 article, "Hemingway, Money, and *The Sun Also Rises,*" agrees with and amplifies the above, then moves on to explain how Hem-

Excerpted from "The Bought Generation: Another Look at Money in *The Sun Also Rises,*" by Patrick D. Morrow, in *Money Talks: Language and Lucre in American Fiction,* edited by Roy R. Male. Copyright © 1981 by the University of Oklahoma Press. Reprinted by permission of the University of Oklahoma Press.

ingway uses financial transactions to reveal Jake as the novel's uncontested moral hero. Finally, in a 1979 article, Nancy Comley proffers a diagrammed schemata "to show how this concern with money manifests itself in an economic structure of exchange values which the Hemingway hero learns to apply to his life, most especially to his emotional relationships." This linear critical development has certainly provided worthwhile insights into the role of money in *The Sun Also Rises,* but the topic is hardly a closed account.

Money is not merely an issue or a revealing metaphorical and moral pattern in *The Sun Also Rises;* money is an obsession in this novel. By my count, *The Sun Also Rises* contains 142 direct references to money, including such varied forms of monetary transactions as paying bills, tipping, betting, bribery, and borrowing and lending, in addition to several metaphorical uses and philosophical discussions of money. ... By my count there are an additional 71 indirect references, such as characters ordering drinks without direct mention of paying for them. In *The Sun Also Rises,* then, there is some kind of monetary reference for every 1.2 pages. Two questions arise at once from this data: what would account for Hemingway's intense concern with money in *The Sun Also Rises,* and what is the meaning of money in this novel? ...

MONEY KEEPS THE CIRCULAR CYCLE OF ENTERTAINMENT ALIVE

Perceived as recurring metaphorical pattern, the monetary references in *The Sun Also Rises* reveal not only a vertical, hierarchical objective correlative to character morality, but also a constant circular, senseless, and frustrating motion by the characters. As such, money is a major component of the novel's circular formal and thematic essence. Its story is about a circle of people who journey in a circle within a circle (Paris, San Sebastian, Bayonne, Pamplona, Burguete, Pamplona, Burguete, Pamplona, San Sebastian, Madrid, Paris). Circular objects, from lights and tables to coins to the bull ring, form much of the setting. Hemingway even puns on this metaphor with his constant references to rounds of drinks. Money establishes the moral dimension of *The Sun Also Rises* as circular.

A whirl of speculation is the order of the day in *The Sun Also Rises.* Despite all the buying and selling of goods, the money spent buys few articles of substance. Expensive and frequent purchases of alcohol lubricate this *La Dolce Vita* world where everybody parties, but no one has any fun. Like alcohol, transportation is purchased for diversion, and throughout the novel there are several aimless taxi cab and automobile rides. At least transportation does provide movement to a new hotel room or café for the old diversions. There are no investments in the novel, and the monetary waste is continual, increasingly appalling as the novel progresses. While the concept of making money is mentioned several times in *The Sun Also Rises,* there is *no* mention of money in terms of future security. Rather, more money ensures that the "entertaining" circular movement of life without purpose can continue.

Several ideas about money recur during the course of *The Sun Also Rises.* One is the idea that money is the way to buy and control friendship. For example, Robert Cohn offers to pay Jake's way to South America. The rich Cohn defines himself largely by using money as magnanimous gesture, a way to obligate, to control. Similarly, Count (another Hemingway pun?) Mippipopolous offers Brett ten thousand dollars if she will accompany him to Biarritz. "The high priest of materialism," as Delbert E. Wylder calls the Count, wishes to join and encumber the younger generation by financial obligation. With more success, Brett buys the friendship of Jake's concierge for two hundred francs. A desperate Pedro Romero presses money on Brett in the hope of establishing physical control and obligation over her. In addition to subsidizing Brett, Jake overtips at a hotel in order to buy the help's friendship in case he should happen to stay there again. Money is the key link among the novel's characters, their primary foundation for establishing relationships.

MONEY DEFINES LITERARY WORTH

Even art and religion are measured in terms of money in *The Sun Also Rises.* Robert Cohn writes, according to Jake, a very bad novel, but ironically Jake is impressed that the book made so much money. Jake also admires Bill Gorton because of all the money he has made on his books. No mention is made about the quality of Gorton's writing. Journalist Jake writes for money to buy time for indulging in seemingly masochistic diversions. Jake, who professes to be Catholic, goes to a church where he quite sincerely prays to make a lot of money. When he mentions money in the prayer, though, he loses track of his prayer (as he has lost track of his faith), and becomes ashamed of himself. The bullfighters Belmonte and Mercial have corrupted their art for money; Romero is the true artist, not connected at all with money—until his encounter with Brett. Most of the characters at one time or another believe in and act on the notion that money purchases exemption from personal and moral responsibilities.

HARRIS BUYS JAKE AND BILL OFF

The only chapter in which money is not a factor is Chapter Twelve, where Jake and Bill go on a fishing trip to Burguete. Money does get mentioned early in the chapter when Bill inquires after he has seen Jake digging for worms, "What were you doing, burying your money?" This is exactly what Jake has done; he buries all mention of money during their trip to the Irati River. Hemingway chooses to show nature as incorrupted in this section, a healing wilderness for troubled men. The stream, as a non-circular encounter between man and nature, is one place where money has no use or value.

This pastoral interlude or counter-action in *The Sun Also Rises* supposedly features the novel's one truly admirable character, Wilson-Harris. He actually functions, however, not as a minor code hero, but as an echo of Jake's worst characteristics. Duplicitous as his name reveals, Wilson-Harris insists on buying friendship with alcohol and gifts. He makes what should be at least for Jake a brutally ironic statement: "I say. You don't know what it's meant to me to have you chaps up here. . . . I've not had much fun since the war." Ever the affected Englishman, fawning continual compliments, Wilson-Harris is defined by his sentimental loneliness. His congeniality masks the magnanimous gestures of a man who pays to keep Jake and Bill for himself. Not surprisingly, Wilson-Harris declines an invitation to return to "civilization" and join the circle for the festival.

THE CHARACTERS USE MONEY TO COMPENSATE FOR THEIR WEAKNESSES

Money serves as a continual means for Hemingway to define and develop his characters within their circles of frustration. Narrator Jake Barnes, mutilated by a grotesque war accident, feels sexual desire, but is physically incapable of having sex. Money appears to be Jake's only means for over-coming his impotence and achieving some measure of power. He pays the majority of the expenses in the book and is also the prime lender; rarely is he repaid in cash. To Lady Brett Ashley, his primary client, he gives all that he possibly can, and is compensated by her off-hand requests for more and more financial support. As the various café scenes indicate, money is typically the medium for their emotional exchanges. Jake even grants money sacred sanction and authority by substituting money for grace in the first church scene. Jake may be so obsessed with money partially because he sees its function in an honest perspective. Without money, he and the other "cult" members would have absolute *nada;* with it, there are at least amusing diversions and some measure of feeling.

Jake's sidekick, Bill Gorton, is more bemused visitor than loyal group member. Only loosely an expatriate, he is also the only member of the party not emotionally involved with Brett. Bill does express some interest in Edna, the tourist and "groupie" picked up in a Pamplona bar. She has known Bill before, and acts most impressed with his apparently independent ways and means. But Bill's real interests and values lie elsewhere. Gorton is a financially successful nature writer, and his behavior at the fiesta demonstrates his eager willingness to enjoy the corruption of civilization and success. Bill's monetary philosophy can best be established by his own words: "Simple exchange of values. You give them money. They give you a stuffed dog." Money equals value; money *is* value.

In Pamplona, Jake continues to buy and Lady Brett enjoys being purchased. Not valuing loyalty very highly, throughout the novel Brett entertains herself by the way a variety of men speculate over her. She uses Robert Cohn and Pedro Romero, and then sells them out by repossessing herself. She uses Mike Campbell as something of a sympatico sponge and reliable sexual toy while maintaining Jake as a crying towel and source of instant income. She could be considered parasitic, living off three men's money in the same careless manner in which she employs their bodies and attentions. Brett is the group's prostitute in that most all her relationships sooner or later become based on money. Her "intended," Mike Campbell, is both a financial and moral bankrupt. He too lives on credit, continually depending on his friends to bail him out of embarrassing situations. A practiced free-loader, Campbell even manages to have Brett pay most of his Pamplona hotel bill. Mike hints that he was cheated monetarily by his former partner, just as in Pamplona he is cheated emotionally by Brett. Mike whines and whines, the complete, even willing professional victim. As deadbeat, Brett takes the opposite tack, protesting loudly against her most insistent emotional and financial creditor, Robert Cohn.

The other two men in Brett's life besides Jake and Mike, Robert Cohn and Pedro Romero, fancy themselves idealists, but actually find their fulfillment as well in being victims. Cohn is a corrupted idealist, smugly believing that no one appreciates his true worth. He plays a system of romantic chivalry with the group, expecting and receiving ridicule and rejection. At the same time, Cohn attempts to proffer money as a way to obligate other characters, and as a way to rid himself of problems, such as how to placate his enraged fiancée in order to have a seacoast fling with Brett. Once again, money resolves a difficult personal and moral situation in *The Sun Also Rises.* The immature Cohn is concerned with appearances and "getting away with it," shunning substantial values at all cost. Of course Cohn, the sad, ineffectual woman-haunted Princetonian, is most debilitated by being a Scott Fitzgerald hero in an Ernest Hemingway novel. As the logical polar opposite to Cohn, Pedro Romero appears at first to be incorrupt and incorruptible. However, he picks up enough of Lost Generation life to realize the potential in Brett's passion for him. When Romero finds that he cannot possess Brett, he finds a mutually agreeable indirect means of payment for services rendered. He, too, comes to know how these expatriates value money.

BRETT CONTROLS HER MEN SEXUALLY WITHOUT ACCEPTING MONEY

The circular movement of money and characters in *The Sun Also Rises* positions Jake and Brett as antagonists at the center in the novel's ring of action. An initiation novel *The Sun Also Rises* is not. Both these antagonists have been wounded, and out of their experiences have developed clearly defined moral codes. Brett believes in and acts on extrinsic values, a code of survival through sensation and appetite. As Brett puts it, "I've always done just what I wanted." Brett values not abstract concepts but what she wants to have. She accepts the depravity of man, exists only in the present tense, lives for disorder and uproar, and, as a creature of process, values most what she cannot have. But Brett also possesses a compelling contrary dimension, a great capacity for nurturing and love, and she is never more human and appealing than when she exhibits this vulnerability.

In terms of character development and values, the issue of money reveals much about Brett Ashley, Jake's formidable love and opponent. Robert Cohn first sees her as a lovely creature resembling Snow White, then views her, with Mike's drunken approval, as Circe. Jake typically sees her as the irresistible tormentor, fate, the bitch goddess. Critics frequently lose objectivity with Brett and empathize with these male characters' feelings about her. For example, Sheridan Baker states that "Brett must have an ever new man [sic] to replace the one she drains," and Robert W. Lewis portrays Brett as the woman in Ecclesiastes whose "heart is snares and nets." Brett, however, has her own values, and it is the males' continual egocentric mistake of substituting their own projections of Brett's identity for her actual identity that causes so much masculine misery in the novel. Highlighted by contrast to Edna and Frances, Lady Brett is defined not by men, but by her own self-validated morality of appetite and survival. Brett is the best and most powerful practitioner of traditional male values, and this strength is nowhere more in evidence than when the males insist on celebrating her as their female goddess. The *riau-riau* establishes Brett's complete control of the situation. Hardly a passive female, alternating between feeling states of male adoration and self-martyrdom, Brett surrounds herself with male strays who define themselves by being dominated victims.

Hemingway is aware of the humor this role-reversal situation can provide. We note the following exchange between Brett and Jake in the Café Select.

> I [Jake] said good night to Brett at the bar. The count [Mippipopolous] was buying champagne. "Will you take a glass with us, sir?" he asked.

> "No. Thanks awfully. I have to go."

> "Really going?" Brett asked.

> "Yes," I said. "I've got a rotten headache."

Jake will come to imitate more than Brett's British speech

mannerisms. Established early in *The Sun Also Rises*, Brett's ability to generate, sustain, and be the center of situation after situation borders on the charismatic. Brett's outrageous behavior, her wardrobe and hair style, her calling herself a "chap," her skill and pride in being a "good drunk," her cavalier assumption that she can always get money—all demonstrate the validity of her strategy that to be a successful female, one must compete to be the most successful male.

Brett seeks not happiness but freedom. To this end she willingly rents herself out to attractive and useful landlords, but she is dominated and bought by no man. True to her values, she never once accepts money as payment for sex. Brett views the prostitute Georgette with scorn, nastily calling Jake's evening with her "restraint of trade." The novel's absorbing and futile quest by the leading male characters to become sole owner of Lady Ashley climaxes with her rejection of Pedro Romero. Like the other males, Romero is capable of seeing only his personal projection of Brett, but not Brett. He wishes to make an honest woman of her, reforming her by means of marriage, motherhood, and long hair. As Brett tells Jake near the end of *The Sun Also Rises:*

> "I didn't know whether I could make him go, and I didn't have a sou to go away and leave him. He tried to give me a lot of money, you know. I told him I had scads of it. He knew that was a lie. I couldn't take his money, you know. . . . He really wanted to marry me. So I couldn't go away from him, he said. He wanted to make it sure I could never go away from him. After I'd gotten more womanly, of course."

Brett typically acts in the plural; she sends for Jake, but plans a return to Mike Campbell. Brett tells Jake she is not a bitch and "It's sort of what we have instead of God" partially because she would like to believe these words, but especially because she likes Jake, is sensitive to his problems, and knows he needs to hear this. More than any character in the novel, Brett has the capability to balance a show of pity and irony. Jake celebrates his quasi-repossession by indulging his appetite and by buying Brett all the booze she can drink and food she can eat. Brett intimidates and disorients the male characters in *The Sun Also Rises* to such an extent that none of them thinks to analyze her motives and behavior with the intention of developing effective strategies for either friendship or revenge.

As Brett's antagonist, Jake, with his capacity for being nurtured, believes in the intrinsic values of the *aficion:* purity and skill are inherently beautiful and good. With a shaky faith, he wants and needs to believe in loyalty, justice, love, and the fundamental good will of mankind. We note the careful accounting of his bank balance, his notion of fair payment, and realize that he is the party of order. But Jake's vulnerability is his contradictory attraction to and need for the dominating Brett Ashley and her values. This vulnerability exists because Jake has been so terribly wounded. A Catholic, however fallen-away, he knows that he must have done something terribly wrong to have received such a punishment. Having no idea what he did to deserve this *corida,* Jake sometimes manufactures evil—betraying Montoya, pimping, getting drunk, acceding to Brett—in an attempt to believe that behind his being wounded, cause and effect firmly stand. Thus, Jake can perceive himself as an evil hero. However sympathetic or admirable, Jake is badly debilitated. This is a Fisher King, not an heroic young knight, that Hemingway sends into the arena to do battle against Duessa.

It *is* rather pleasant to think that after the fiesta, Jake recovers his lost values while vacationing in San Sebastian, so that when he encounters Brett in Madrid, he has come to his senses with a self-awareness born out of tragic recognition, and can rise above further involvement in her romantic conspiracies. As we have seen, such forms the prevailing critical view. Hemingway himself insisted that *The Sun Also Rises* was not a satire but a tragedy. If Hemingway's book follows the tragic novel convention of a fallen, wounded hero rising to self-knowledge, a morally admirable perspective, and a consequent series of actions, then Jake must be congratulated for achieving an heroic stature in the *dénouement.* However, partially through the money metaphor, Hemingway undercuts this uplifting pattern to reveal not an emerging hero, but a continuation of frustration in this world where extrinsic values dominate. Drunk in Pamplona, Jake muses about money and life, ending his reverie by stating: "Maybe if you found out how to live in it you learned from that what it was all about." Jake comes to realize that "how to live in it" (extrinsic values, i.e., money) and "what it was all about" (intrinsic values, i.e., honor) are at irreconcilable odds. . . . Jake resigns himself to being overwhelmed by a stronger force (Brett). Hemingway's pronouncement on *The Sun Also Rises* as a tragedy rings true when we realize the tragedy of the novel is that Jake cannot act on his beliefs. Typical of the twentieth-century American novelist, Hemingway saves most of the blow from this realization not for his protagonist, but for his audience.

IN THE END, JAKE'S STILL PAYING

In the opening of Part III, the scene immediately following the Pamplona festival's ending, Jake makes a number of decisions that indicate not resolve or enlightenment, but a serious depression. First of all, he determinedly insists on staying alone in San Sebastian, the scene of the earlier Cohn-Ashley "crime." Interestingly, although Jake notes that he has been to this hotel before, he never names the hotel, possibly because while there, Jake acts like a sanitarium patient rather than a spa vacationer. Jake is comforted by watching the visiting nurses, immediately imposes a daily routine of therapeutic swimming and sitting, and refuses to join the community of bicycle racers. Jake's self-absorption is overwhelming. Typical of institutional life, meals constitute the high points of his days. He acts drugged and tense, at the edge of breakdown. . . . Jake's languid days of isolated insulation do afford protection against the outside world of Spain, where "you could not tell about anything." His regrets about returning to Spain concern consequences, phrased in a nostalgic financial metaphor about France.

> Everything is on such a clear financial basis in France. It is the simplest country to live in. No one makes things complicated by becoming your friend for any obscure reason. If you want people to like you you have only to spend a little money.

When Brett's telegrams arrive, Jake laments "that meant San Sebastian all shot to hell." This expression of surprise is an act. Having learned from Mike Campbell that Brett is broke, Jake knows that she will be in touch with him shortly. Certainly Jake could wire Brett to go to hell and continue his quasi-hospitalization, but like an heroic rescue agent, he rushes to her aid at once. Again, action is "put on the bill." What Brett does need is a paying audience. Page after page she has demonstrated her ability to rescue herself.

Far from establishing a clean, well-lighted place of heroic action for Jake, the final scene ironically demonstrates the novel's enduring French values: *plus ça change, plus c'est la même chose.* What does the last scene change except location? In Madrid, Jake still pays and Brett still buys. When

Jake first meets Brett in the sleazy Hotel Montana, he notes that her "room was in that disorder produced only by those who have always had servants." Jake continues his role of servant par excellence by patiently listening to Brett's sad tale of her latest affair; by paying for drinks and meals; and by booking them on the Sud Express for a night trip back to Paris. Jake would have paid for Brett's room, but Romero has already made this contribution as Brett's severance payment. At Botin's, "one of the best restaurants in the world," Brett becomes concerned with Jake's sudden conspicuous consumption (including five bottles of *rioja alta*), fearing another unpleasant scene of drunken, weepy pouting. Brett soothes by words but abuses by actions, a much more effective strategy for achieving her goals than the explosion of verbal indictment that Frances practices. In the end, both Jake and Robert Cohn "take it." The final tipping, the furtive taxi ride, and that hideously ironic upraised baton of the mounted policeman establish at the novel's finalé not a sense of recognition or resolution, but a continuing wandering. Like Francesca and Paolo, swept on hot winds without touching through their circle of Dante's Hell, Jake and Brett are driven through summertime Madrid on the winds of money. Instead of establishing security in space, money in *The Sun Also Rises* is most useful for killing time. Rather than establishing superiority or even disengagement, Jake capitulates by joining Brett and her extrinsic values of meaningless motion and immediate gratification.

Mortgaged to Frustration

The use of money, then, is a major means for Hemingway to show the corruption of this modern world where values are relative, transitory, and for sale. Far from praising this lost generation, Hemingway damns their meaningless exchanges and lack of purpose, the absence of a moral center in their world. He attacks their irresponsibility by dramatizing their fruitless, circular quests for happy diversions. Jake requires diversion to forget his faded Catholicism and his painfully impotent love for Brett. Brett requires diversion to cover up her exploitations and encroaching middle age. Mike needs diversion because he is both a moral and financial bankrupt; diversions occupy his time and give some vague sense of direction to his life, namely a moving on to wherever he can still obtain credit. While a means, money is not—as Bill

Gorton claims—an end in *The Sun Also Rises*. Despite the many equations of money to value in the book, money is not in itself valuable to the characters, but only the means for continuing their dissipation. If money is not a value in itself, if it is not a center for *this* group, then Hemingway's characters literally have lost all values. Far from being hostages to fortune, these characters, however wounded, create their own tragedy and hell.

The Sun Also Rises is a cyclical, cynical young man's book. Jake, Brett, and, by insinuation, Mike are the only characters left at the end of the novel because, in spite of their singular and collective guilt, they all accept and function well in the never-ending cycle of borrowing on time. Neither of the romantics, Robert Cohn and Pedro Romero, ever comprehends this cycle: they are both idealists, albeit corrupt ones. Bill Gorton is eliminated from the cycle because he is only a visiting expatriate, soon off to America. The concept of "paying the bill" works in tandem with the novel's cyclical process. Jake pays for his impotence and loss of religion; Brett pays for her manipulative behavior; Mike, Cohn and Romero pay for thinking they can possess Brett; Mike pays for his insolvent status; Cohn pays for behaving badly; Bill Gorton pays for his stagnancy. All the characters pay for their lack of purpose, their lack of definite goals, and their values which center around vanities.

Payment in *The Sun Also Rises* is not rendered in such concrete terms as cold cash; rather, the characters are mortgaged to frustration. As this cyclical pattern indicates, appropriately consummated by Jake's tipping a waiter and ordering a taxi as the novel closes, these characters can never gain on their moral deficit, but shall continue, gradually and voluntarily, to slide into the self-destruction of a material and moral receivership.

Social Class in *The Sun Also Rises*

Marc D. Baldwin

Marc D. Baldwin teaches composition and literature
at Hillsborough Community College in Tampa,
Florida, and has published articles on William
Faulkner, F. Scott Fitzgerald, and popular culture.
Here he shows how class consciousness imbues
each of the characters with a need to dominate the
rest, with Brett obviously this dictum's most successful proponent. No matter how reprehensible their
acts, the characters, by virtue of their "breeding,"
are beyond real reproach from each other.

Ernest Hemingway's *The Sun Also Rises* [hereafter referred
to as *SAR*] has endured a variety of readings over the years,
but few have investigated its social and ideological matrix.
"To understand an ideology we must understand the precise
relations between different classes in a society," argues
Terry Eagleton. Ideology imparts and reflects what Georg
Lukacs calls a "class consciousness," succinctly defined by
Fredric Jameson as "the a priori limits or advantages con-
ferred by affiliation with the bourgeoisie or the proletariat
upon the mind's capacity to apprehend external reality." The
narrator of *SAR*, Jake Barnes, seems ideologically bound
and determined to "apprehend" his "external reality" as a
struggle for control and dominance over individuals belonging to other classes.

SAR bristles with examples of this class consciousness:
the Jew Cohn and his exclusion from Brett's "us"; the hundreds of anonymous workers serving Jake and his "gang";
the many titles (Duke, Count, Lady, Baron, boxing champion,
President) and their nature and significance; and the obsessive notation of "class," "breeding," "royalty," "aristocracy,"
"gentry," "her own people," and "one of us." Even prostitutes

Excerpted from "Class Consciousness and the Ideology of Dominance in *The Sun Also
Rises*," by Marc D. Baldwin, *The McNeese Review*, vol. 33, pp. 14–32 (1990–1994).
Reprinted with permission.

discriminate and defer only to a perceived superior authority or class. Georgette immediately dislikes Frances Clyne, sensing her artificiality: "Georgette turned to me. 'Do I have to talk to her?'" She knows the protocol, asking her evening's master for permission to ignore an annoying inferior. Significantly, the clash of contradictory classes is revealed through their differing perspectives of Paris: Frances "find[s] it so extraordinarily clean," while the street walker "find[s] it dirty."

Clearly, the narration reveals a *consciousness of class,* whatever the "class consciousness" may be. Jake and Brett are constantly rating, calculating, scrutinizing, and categorizing others as belonging to one ethnic group or another. The origin or cause of this behavior is overdetermined by the practices of their society. In part, their consciousness of class is a defense mechanism born of the war wound: the world is divided into "us" and "them," and "friends" and "enemies." Class consciousness also mimics the economic production process, fragmenting and breaking down the various factions of society into ever smaller and more manageable ethnic groups. In their consciousness of class, Jake and Brett are simply responding naturally according to their congenital class consciousness. This indigenous instinct to classify and compete constitutes one of the poignant contradictions of the dominant ideology: democracy touts harmony and equality, yet the majority rules, and those privileged by birth, property, or a superior income control the structure of society and dominate the "lower" classes.

CLASS DELINEATIONS AMONG JAKE'S FRIENDS ARE FAST AND LOOSE

Any attempt to "rate" the various individuals and groups in the text into classes demonstrates the inherent contradictions and ultimate subjectivity of such hierarchical structuring. There is no clear common denominator, line of demarcation, or logical differentiation between natural and social "class" or dominance. The peasants would seem to be on the bottom of the scale, yet they are rooted in the earth and have a natural dignity that most of their "superiors" lack. Above them on the social scale are the anonymous workers—drivers, waiters, manual laborers—who also earn a living and thus are entitled to respect. Jake does not at all disparage the *poules,* seemingly admiring their professionalism and placing Georgette, at least, above such pompous socialites as

Frances and even Mrs. Braddocks, who "was a Canadian and had all their easy social graces." Decidedly above the preceding are Brett's set: Mike, Bill, and Jake himself. Somewhat on an even level, but laterally displaced, are the English tourist Harris and the Spanish aficionado Montoya. The anomalies in this class equation are Cohn—because he qualifies for the upper classes monetarily and socially, but not ethnically—and Romero—who, although a peasant, has reached the status of a prince, a national hero and idol. It is these two "hybrids" who rival Jake and cause him the most anxiety, apprehension, and jealousy in his own identity crisis. There are also the absent "gentry," "aristocrats," and "royalty" who hover overhead as ubiquitous reminders of one's own relatively low station. By these narrative specifications Jake means to imply that there are "classes," yet the many deviations from strict categories subvert the very notion of an "us" or a "people." Furthermore, "classes" do not insure that one has *class*—Mike and Brett behave somewhat less than admirably—nor do titles either *entitle* or prove authenticity. The social hierarchy, based on "breeding" and money, does not necessarily correspond to the natural *class* exhibited by those simple people who work hard for a living and assume no pretentious airs of superiority.

In the early twentieth century, these "assumed superiorities of the genteel tradition" were "converted [by] institutionalized expectations of economic growth and a rising standard of living . . . into a sense of *entitlements*." In *SAR*, those with the most developed sense of entitlements have titles, and the only "significant" titles in the novel are those bestowed by the state (president) or the fourth estate (editor and publisher). Brett acquires her "Lady" title by marriage, a dubious designation at best and as suspect as the other three titled characters—the count and his friends, the duke and the baron. They all represent the false aristocracy of the *nouveau riche*. Zizi, a "little Greek portrait-painter . . . only called himself a duke," says Jake, and the baron raises grapes. Skeptical of titles, Jake asks Brett:

"Is he a count?"

"Here's how. I rather think so, you know. Deserves to be, anyhow. Knows hell's own amount about people. Don't know where he got it all. Owns a chain of sweetshops in the States. . . . He's one of us, though. Oh, quite. No doubt. One can always tell."

Brett believes that the count "deserves to be" a count, whether he is or not, because he knows "about people." The count certainly knows about her: he spends money on her and she is impressed. . . .

THE COUNT IS A POSEUR

The count is given away by his language—his tongue. Pompously puffing on his cigar, the count announces to Brett:

> "You don't need a title. You got class all over you."

> "Thanks. Awfully decent of you."

> "I'm not joking you," the count blew a cloud of smoke. "You got the most class of anybody I ever seen. You got it. That's all."

One who has "class" does not talk about it. Furthermore, both Hemingway and Jake know the difference between "you got" and "you've got," and "I ever seen" and "I've ever seen." They are both consummate artists and aficionados of dialect: grammar and diction are indicators of class. The "nigger drummer" greets Brett with "Hahre you?" When Brett answers, "Great," he replies, "Thaats good." A "German maitre d'hôtel," who Jake and Bill believe is "damned snotty" (a sign of class consciousness), also talks *differently:* "'Iss madam eating here?' 'No,' Brett said. 'Den I think a tabul for two will be enuff.'" Like the emperor who wore no clothes, the count's faulty grammar exposes him as a fraud, effectively *discounting* and declassifying him.

One wonders, then, what a title is worth and what a title confers.

> "Isn't it wonderful," said Brett. "We all have titles. Why haven't you a title, Jake?"

> "I assure you, sir," the count put his hand on my arm. "It never does a man any good. Most of the time it costs you money."

> "Oh, I don't know. It's damned useful sometimes," Brett said.

> "I've never known it to do me any good."

> "You haven't used it properly. I've had hell's own amount of credit on mine."

As the count is wont to do, he is "blowing smoke" again: his title may cost him money, but not only does he relish spending money; such a denial of his title's value also artfully increases the ostensible value of his own *self-worth.* Similar to his conspicuous consumption and his airs of superiority, the count again is complimenting and pampering himself.

BRETT THE HIGH-CLASS TRAMP

Brett, however, frankly and ironically admits that a title is ". . . damned useful" if "used . . . properly." She has turned her title to profit, exchanged it for whatever the market will bear: "I've had hell's own amount of credit on mine." Lady Brett—who will lose her title when divorced and about whose birth we know nothing—and her current fiancé, Mike—who has no title, yet is the only genuine aristocrat among the group—both specialize in living on credit. They are professional borrowers. That the two characters with the most social "class" are the biggest freeloaders in the book speaks silent volumes about the contradictions of the economic system. When one makes it to the top, one can live on credit alone, on the power of a title, parentage, or a promissory note. These people do not work; people work for them.

Ever the exploiter, Brett lives on the credit established by her country's system of monarchic rule: "We ought to toast something. 'Here's to royalty,'" she says. Her spontaneous reaction is to celebrate the class consciousness that has allowed her to live on its credit, sustaining both her finances and her reputation. Since her social position has already been established, she leads a privileged life of entitlements and credit. If she were not "a lady of title," if she were not apparently "of very good family," if she did not appear to have the "breeding" of the "upper classes," by her actions Brett would be considered a woman of "low class," perhaps even a "tramp." She sleeps around; she is vulgar; she is disloyal to Mike; she is lazy and late; she lies when it accommodates her; and she is rude whenever it suits her. She simply is not a "lady" in the traditional sense of a woman with "breeding." Yet, except in the case of Cohn, even her promiscuity is forgiven: "What if Brett did sleep with you?" Mike tells Cohn. "She's slept with lots of better people than you." Mike can excuse her sleeping with "better people": "Brett's gone off with men. But they weren't ever Jews." When it comes to matters of class consciousness, even Bill, the usually iconoclastic subverter of conventions, concurs that Brett lowered herself by sleeping with Cohn: "Why didn't she go off with some of her own people?" One's class is one's "own people." As Brett said, "Michael's people have loads of money." Montoya, too, bows to conventions of ethnic difference and the separation of classes: "'He's such a fine boy,' said Montoya. 'He ought to stay with his own people.'" To "his own people," Romero represents royalty, the entitled torero. . . .

COHN IS NOT "ONE OF US"

As something of a utopian society, a "promised land," Brett attracts the disaffected and displaced expatriates to her shores. Her "totality" called "us" is a linguistic tool of dominance and oppression, an imaginary principle which both ties the text to ideology, and distances the text from ideology: Brett has appropriated her resources and title as a means of expropriating others. Thoroughly conscious of class and utterly determined to classify and exclude those who do not measure up, Brett constructs "us" as a centering device, what Louis Althusser calls an Absolute Subject that "recruits," "hails," or "interpellates" others into concrete subjects. Specific criteria exist by which Jake, the count, and Romero are "hailed" by Brett's "us," while Cohn is rejected.

Class counts, of course, yet membership is not simply determined or denied by ethnicity. Cohn's Jewishness is a factor in his rejection, but the narration clearly implies that had his personality been less grating, had he not "hung around" and just "looked at Brett," and had he not "behaved badly," he might have been accepted by the group. In other words, not every Jew is as offensive as "that kike" Cohn. An individual's work and income is important, but again, like ethnicity, not a determining factor. Mike and Brett live on credit, yet they are never criticized. The peasants and drivers and waiters and most of the other workers in the story all earn their own money, yet they are never considered even remotely eligible for admittance into "us." Brett tells Jake about the count's "chain of sweetshops," concluding that "He's one of us, though." Her "though" seems to imply that *despite* being a businessman, the count is "one of us." That would be consistent with Brett's capitalistic code: the count is a working man, yet he is a wealthy owner and thus superior. One must also exhibit an ideological individuality to obtain admittance into the coterie. The miscellaneous peasants and workers all seem homogenous; groups of people populate the narrative. Only a few individuals stand out from the crowd: Brett by her flaunting of the conventional standards of femininity, Bill by his ironic lampooning of the status quo, Montoya by his dignified presence and integrity, Harris by his genuine good fellowship, and Romero by his professional and charismatic bearing. Individuals must have a strong sense not only of themselves, but also of the body politic. Cohn does not: "If he were in a crowd nothing he said stood out." Thus, the operative principle of inclusion or exclusion by Brett's "us" seems to be a combination of the three elements—a structural causality composed of ethnicity, economic independence, and individuality. One must possess some measure of all three in order to be considered "one of us." But there is also a fourth factor that cannot be overlooked in determining one's eligibility: the wound.

Brett has been wounded by the war: losing her one true love, then marrying the "Ashley chap," who made her sleep on the floor and threatened to kill her. When the count shows off his arrow wounds and reports that he received them while "on a business trip," Brett replies, "I told you he was one of us." Again, this seems contradictory, for to receive one's wounds as a soldier in war is not the same as receiving them while on a "business trip." Yet, since they are attained accidentally, the count's wounds represent humankind's helplessness against the forces of fate and *nada*. Thus the count qualifies as "one of us" because he risks the maximum exposure and has been wounded while going about his professional business. Although Jake's wound differs significantly from Brett's and the count's, it represents the one trait shared by all three: class and commodity consciousness. All three were wounded by a war *waged* (as are all wars) over class and commodities, for the spoils of mastery and domination: when Brett's first husband was killed in battle, she was further wounded by marrying a man she didn't love, presumably for his money and title; the count was wounded in a battle for business in a war zone; and Jake was wounded in an unspecified manner while playing an unspecified role in the conflict. Of the three, Jake's war wound is at once the most undeserved, the most devastating, and the most influential upon his character. Jake's wound becomes the novel's premise which determines so much of his ideology and behavior. Because of his wound, Jake cannot be one with Brett, nor can he ever reproduce or ever feel whole or one with himself. His wound heightens the significance of his male bonding with Bill and, more importantly, his attraction to and obsession with *toreo* and its cult of *afición*. . . .

TOREO: THE STRUGGLE FOR DOMINANCE BETWEEN MAN AND BEAST

As a ritual, *toreo* is a living embodiment of ideology, a "representation of the imaginary relationship of individuals to the real conditions of their existence." Hemingway's (and Jake's) glorification of *toreo* reveals a desire for the ideological lie, a need to cover the base *real* of material existence with a superstructural *imaginary* of some ideal fantasy. . . .

As a tool of containment, *toreo* perniciously appropriates idealism itself to mythologize the lie that everyone can be like a matador. *Toreo* celebrates the matador with the best form, who best conceals his devices, who has, as it were, the most invisible ideology and makes the act of domination appear the most natural and easiest to affect. It is not enough merely to dominate the bull; one must dominate the bull effortlessly, as if one is entitled to do so by the "purity of his line." The one with the idea(l)s that society has accepted—those idea(l)s of social position: style, grace, bearing, class, manners, form, integrity, and so on—conquers both the bull and the people. This imposition of imperialism—this breeding, exploitation, penetration, and domination of bulls, people, and countries—effaces itself behind the graceful veil of an obfuscating ideology such as religion or *toreo*.

Ultimately, Jake has painted a portrait of *toreo* and its aficionados as a cult. Although he makes an effort to pray and to believe, Jake is clearly disillusioned by Catholicism's failure to redress his wound and to offer a totalizing myth that would counteract the outside world's decadence and chaos. "Where religions fail, cults appear." In the bullfight ring, Jake shares in a "communal rite" celebrating "tabooed modes of conduct" that satisfy his "hunger for ritual, and myth." C.W.E. Bigsby neatly encapsulizes Jake's and most critics' consensual interpretation of the attraction of *toreo:*

> The bullfight is important because, though an artificial construct, it offers an ordered experience in which it is possible to distinguish the authentic from the sham, the true from the merely plausible. The bullfighter, true to the standards and traditions of his craft, like the writer anxious to strip his work of all pretence and dishonesty, is pitching himself against both a form of spiritual decadence and the constant threat of dissolution. He challenges death, the final anarchic impulse. He challenges the principle of disorder, creating a discrete universe, outside of time, in which control, personal courage and purity of style have a meaning denied the indi-

vidual faced with the anti-tragic banalities of the modern wasteland.

This agenda of bullfighting resembles that of a religion or a cult: to provide the people with "an ordered experience" that defines what is "true" and counteracts the world's "spiritual decadence" and "disorder," leading them to a "discrete universe, outside of time"—a heaven on earth, so to speak. Such utopian depiction of *toreo* concomitantly implies that the present state of life outside the cult has become meaningless. Ironically, such an ideological position is self-referentially Marxist: the cult of *toreo* that Jake so reveres is a model of anti-capitalist social communism.

KILL YOUR BEST FRIENDS BEFORE THEY KILL YOU

Like the capitalist societies they so mimic even as they renounce, *toreo,* social communism, and the characters of *SAR* have all fallen prey to the inevitably corrupting force of power itself. In dominating one is dominated, for the precedent once set assures an illimitable succession of competitive struggles. Once having been on top, Belmonte is now topped by Romero. Cohn, having topped Brett, must topple off Brett and be topped by his successor. Brett, now on top, is 34 years old and will soon be toppled from her throne, if not by younger beauties, then by age itself. Lovers, presidents, governments, states, and nations: all that dominate have been or will be dominated. Such is the plight of humankind.

That rude truth is the essence of the "shocking" and "lewd" secret between aficionados: that because violent domination is the fate of all creatures, why not celebrate, ritualize, mythologize, and spectacularize it? Why not make a show of it, reproduce it, sell it, make money on it, commodify and package it? But only "expose" its truth to those who "understand," for most people cannot resist the fatal truth of their own animality. *Toreo* lays claim to the esoteric knowledge of man's bestiality, a knowledge denied and scorned by orthodox religions and outsiders such as Cohn, who is "afraid I may be bored" by the bullfight, and the waiter, who, angered by the death of Vincent Girones, says: "What are bulls? Animals. Brute animals." If one is bored by *toreo,* one is bored by life; the fight with the bull is not merely man against animal. It is species against species, gender against gender, race against race, and class against class. The butcher-priest's final thrust that kills the bull is at once sexual and social, a gender and an ethnic expropriation and execution. Animals prey upon and devour *other* species; human beings prey upon and devour *other* animals, sexes, and classes. After all, Romero admits with a laugh that he "always" kills his "best friends," the bulls, "So they don't kill me." *Toreo* as ideology reflects the reality (at least for Hemingway and Jake) that living creatures are by nature divided, classified, opposed, and adversarial. The "really very deep secret" that Jake and Montoya share is the knowledge that all men and women are animals and, like animals, they are engaged in nature's violent struggle for social dominance.

The 1920s and *The Sun Also Rises*

Michael S. Reynolds

Though the dialogue and values of Jake and the rest of the characters seem timely and accessible enough to modern readers, Michael S. Reynolds cautions us that the novel is the product of a specific, bygone era. Though the decade *The Sun Also Rises* describes is now equated with "roaring" good times and a party atmosphere, it was also, as Hemingway observed, a time of dizzying consumerism, racial prejudice sanctioned as patriotism, and "moral" crusaders. To read the novel without this awareness is to grossly miss the novel's point and its timeless bite. Michael S. Reynolds is professor of English at North Carolina State University and the author of three seminal books on Hemingway, including *The Young Hemingway* and *Hemingway's First War*.

More than a half century has now passed since we saw the first light of Hemingway's *The Sun Also Rises*—a half century of bloody war and remarkable change: the jet age, the atomic age, the computer age. Next summer at Pamplona the grandchildren of the twenties will make the pilgrimage, looking under the Irunia arcade for an experience trapped in time. In Paris they will sip their beers under the red and gold awnings of the Dome, imagining faces long since gone under the earth. Great books have a way of doing that to us, a way of stopping time. Nostalgia is infectious and easily forgiven. But critics should know better. The places and the weather may look the same, but all else has changed. The music has changed. The clothes have changed. The prices, the moods, the politics, the values—all irrevocably changed. Brett Ashley and Jake Barnes are no longer our contemporaries. Hemingway, as he said of Henry James, is as dead as he will ever be; to continue to read his first novel as if it were written for our age is to be hopelessly romantic.

The Sun's timeless quality, of course, encourages such behavior, but to persist at it past the point of diminished returns is to devalue the novel. *The Sun Also Rises* is a period piece, a historical artifact as precisely dated as that frozen moment at Pompeii. The year is 1925 as it was in another country. The book could not have been written any earlier, for the Great War had not yet produced the war-wounded generation that peoples *The Sun*. A decade later it would not have been written; in the middle of the Great Depression, no one was interested in boozy expatriates. We can no more properly read *The Sun Also Rises* outside of its social and historical context than we can view Picasso's "Les Demoiselles d'Avignon" as if it were painted last year. Both are works of art anchored in time. To treat either artist as if he were our contemporary is to pretend that we are living in an earlier age. Foolishness, utterly. Our time is not their time. Historically blind readers see only the timeless qualities of the work, and even those they are reading at a discount. . . .

Each generation, of course, will read *The Sun* through its own prevailing filter, finding there its own needs. The beat generation of the fifties thought the Paris-Pamplona lifestyle admirable, an early version of *On the Road*. The romantic revolutionaries in the sixties related to Hemingway's war-wounded band of revelers as fellow travelers rejecting the false values of a corrupt society. The conservatives of the eighties, on the other hand, find little to admire in the novel. They condone neither Brett's promiscuity nor Cohn's hopeless romantic ideals. For this present generation, *The Sun Also Rises* is a study in moral failure, a jaded world of unemployed and irresponsible characters who drink too much—a fable of ideological bankruptcy. Ironically, this present age is closer to Hemingway's original view than most of us realize. . . .

A TIME OF PLENTY

Wherever Hemingway looked in 1925, he saw dollar signs. Everything was for sale, its price clearly marked. At the postwar conferences—Versailles, Genoa, Lausanne—the future of Europe was on the auction block. At home, sons of bankers married Follies stars who sold their svelte bodies for immediate returns. The Teapot Dome scandal took Harry

Sinclair and the Standard Oil Company to court: A simple exchange of values—Harry had given the secretary of the interior money in exchange for the navy's oil reserves. Meanwhile, the banker Mellon, as secretary of the treasury, was protecting his own companies from paying federal taxes. Easy money. Quick money. Bootlegger money. In 1923 the tax returns showed 74 millionaires, but those were only the ones who declared honest income. The Paris *Tribune* headlines kept the young writer's nose rubbed in the money pot:

U.S. PROSPERITY IS
GREATEST IN HISTORY

Hoover Credits "Era Of Good Times"
To High Wages, Steady Employment
Wall Street Prices Soar

(November 8, 1925)

The bull market roared and the dollar climbed, peaking that fall at 26 francs when a half franc bought a mug of beer, 1.65 francs bought a loaf of bread, and 800 francs rented a furnished flat for a month. Americans flowed into Paris, changing everything. By early 1924, 100,000 English-speaking residents crowded the city; during the summer season their number doubled. On the Left and Right banks, Americans were everywhere. They could be seen "on any night of July or August packing the Dome or the Dingo or the Select. . . . the most conspicuous one is the flapper who has skipped school and come to see 'life' and the corresponding pink-cheeked, well-scrubbed college boy" (*Tribune*, August 23, 1925). More and more clubs, bars, and dancings opened up to water the crowd, to cater to American money. Prices went up, gentrifying the old bohemian way of life. In the Latin Quarter, fewer and fewer real artists and writers did decent work. . . .

THE FIRST GENERATION OF TECHNOLOGICAL CONSUMERS

As the first wave of consumer technology hit the marketplace, Americans were hard put to keep up with the myriad new devices. By 1923, Henry Ford and his peers were parking 4 million new automobiles in front of American homes. Across the country vaudeville theaters were converting to movie houses. Everything was modern; everything was electric: sewing machines, refrigerators, radios, hair dryers, vacuum cleaners, phonographs, toasters. By 1927 half of the American households owned a record player, a car, and a telephone. We had become a nation of consumers, paying for the new technology in installments. Debt became a way of life in the rush to buy now, live now. American readers, who found Hemingway's novel so lacking in positive moral values, were themselves the willing participants in the nation's first great buying binge. If money seems the only significant value in *The Sun Also Rises*, Hemingway did not create that moral climate, nor does Jake Barnes approve of those who live on the financial brink. "The bill always came," he tells us. "That was one of the swell things you could count on."

Hemingway's Oak Park background never allowed him to despise money. He did not subscribe to any romantic notions about the starving artist, not in those days. In his dotage he might say that hunger was good for the writer, but in those early Paris days, when he was never truly poor, he intended to make a decent living from his writing. Money per se was not corrupting so long as one worked for it. The Americans and British in Paris were not working; that was the burr that galled him. The readers offended by *The Sun Also Rises* did not see that Jake Barnes was equally offended. Because of Jake's reticence, we hear only his understated and ironic bitterness. In 1926, three years away from the money bubble's bursting, Hemingway, like Fitzgerald, had his finger on the sick pulse of an era about to fail. *Hold him in your arms and you can feel his disease*, as the children of a later generation chanted.

THE BAD OLD DAYS

The novel may not be tragic, but it does capture a time and place, reflecting accurately the failings of an age. At least one reviewer understood that "any country's condition can be deduced from the vice and virtues of the expatriates. In them the native attributes are in excess." Today historians and sociologists frequently quote *The Sun* to emphasize the moral dither of those postwar years. Beneath the humorous banter of Bill Gorton, we catch allusions to the American scene, allusions now largely lost on the reader. Today our concept of the twenties has been too thoroughly clouded by Hollywood images of gangsters, speakeasies, short skirts, blaring jazz, and polished automobiles. We have forgotten how reactionary the period actually was.

As Bill and Jake fish above Burguete, Bill makes anachronistic jokes about the death of William Jennings Bryan, the Great Commoner who had become a right-wing, moral reactionary. In 1925 at the Scopes Monkey Trial in Tennessee, fundamentalist Bryan aided the successful prosecutor in upholding the state's law against the teaching of evolution. In the middle of the 1925 Pamplona festival, the Paris *Tribune* headline read:

BRYAN OPENS ATTACK
AT SCOPES TRIAL

Proclaiming "Fight to Death" Against Evolution,
Silver-Tongued Orator Gets Ovation at Dayton

(July 9, 1925)

Today we think of the Scopes trial as an anomaly. It was not. What happened in Tennessee was symptomatic of what was happening in the country. After the corrupt Harding administration, the voters put another Republican, Coolidge, in the White House with a larger plurality than any before in American history. In Congress the first Equal Rights Amendment for women failed; they had the vote—enough was enough. In August 1925, those same congressmen watched 100,000 Ku Klux Klansmen parade down Pennsylvania Avenue dressed in white sheets, their hoods hanging down behind them. No need to hide their faces in the American twenties. On some college campuses, the KKK was just another student organization.

In a 1923 article warning against the *potential* crimes of the Ku Klux Klan, the *New Republic* understood perfectly the mood of white America:

> The Ku Klux Klan holds that the dearest values in American life are Protestantism; white supremacy, in America and the world; Anglo-Saxon legal institutions; the system of free private enterprise. . . . These are respectable values.

The menace was clear:

> Jews and Catholics . . . are steadily gaining by natural increase. Both are advancing in economic power, the Jews especially; both are winning political power, especially the Catholics. . . . the yellow race is taking Hawaii and the Negro race does not look forward to an indefinite period of political exclusion in the South. . . . And as for the enemies of free enterprise and private property, their number is certainly considerable. (January 17, 1923, p. 189)

Jake Barnes is not reassured when Bill Gorton tells him that everything is swell in the States. Jake, like his creator Hemingway, reads the magazines and papers.

Those were the years when a nation whose entire population traced its roots to immigrants began to fear foreigners. Burned by Wilson's idealism in the Great War, America burrowed into an isolationist policy and its first red scare. The Bolsheviks, as if they did not have enough problems in Russia, were said to be plotting the overthrow of our way of life. Socialism was just another name for Communism, and labor unions were thought to be its leading advocates. During the twenties, union membership fell by half; political ideas became dangerous. By 1924 in California, ninety-six men were in state prisons, convicted of political beliefs contrary to the majority view. On the heels of the 1919 Palmer Acts, which deported politically undesirable aliens, the U.S. Congress in 1924 passed the National Origins Act, which limited European immigration by a quota system and totally excluded all Asians. The 1925 U.S. Army war games, staged in Hawaii, were an exercise in defending the islands from a hypothetical Japanese invasion. The next war, many were certain, would be fought against the "yellow horde." In Boston, meanwhile, two Italian immigrants—Sacco and Vanzetti, convicted on questionable evidence of a capital crime—were under sentence of death, victims of the times. The ironic phrase "One Hundred Percent American" became part of our lexicon. Bill Gorton tells Jake, "Fake European standards have ruined you." Bill means it as a joke. At home it was no joke. *The American Mercury,* with the emphasis on *American,* satirized the cosmopolitan with his foreign tastes:

> The smart American drinks St. Emilion, Graves, St. Julien and Macon, the beverages of French peasants. He plays Mah Jong, the game of Chinese coolies. He wears, on Sundays, a cutaway coat, the garb of English clerks. His melodic taste is for jazz, the music of African niggers. He eats alligator pears, the food of Costa Rican billy goats.

The American scene, of which Hemingway's first readers were a part, was filled with fears and prejudices, all in the name of nationalism.

Not the least of those fears was the virulent strain of anti-Semitism that broke out in America after the Great War. Today we remember Hitler's "final solution" for the Jewish question and are appalled. We have conveniently forgotten auto maker Henry Ford and his Dearborn *Independent,* which spewed out a steady stream of Jew-baiting sewage. We have forgotten the "Protocols of the Elders of Zion," a trumped-up anti-Semitic document purporting to be the Jews' master plan to take over Western civilization. We have forgotten Harvard President Abbott Lawrence Lowell's "solution" to widespread anti-Semitism on the college campuses of the twenties. He said:

> There is most unfortunately a rapidly growing anti-Semitic feeling in this country. The question for those of us who deplore such a state of things is how it can be combatted. If every college in the country would take a limited proportion of Jews, I suspect we should go a long way toward eliminating race feeling among the students.

To read *The Sun Also Rises* right, we must remember something of those times.

BRETT'S UNFORGIVABLE SIN

The first thing Jake tells us about Cohn is that he is a Jew who went to Princeton, where a boxing match "certainly improved his nose." Cohn, we hear, "was a member, through his father, of one of the richest Jewish families in New York, and through his mother of one of the oldest." The American reader in 1926 would have picked up those signals: Cohn belonged to the Jewish establishment, which many thought to be a threat to the American way of life. Jake tries to like Cohn but finds him a boor, just as we do today, for Robert Cohn has plenty of dislikable characteristics without his Jewishness being part of the issue. But it is there. Jake never lets the reader forget it. When Cohn first sees Brett Ashley, Jake says he "looked a great deal as his compatriot must have looked when he first saw the promised land." When Cohn says that Jake is the best friend he has, Jake thinks to himself, "God help you." Jake, badly hurt when Brett takes Cohn with her for a week at San Sebastian, does not resort to Jew baiting, but his friends do. Bill wonders, "Why didn't she go off with some of her own people?" And Mike says, "Brett's gone off with men. But they weren't Jews." Brett's promiscuity they can forgive, but not her choice of a Jew.

Readers today are apt to say that Hemingway's depiction of Robert Cohn betrays his anti-Semitism, which it does—the same anti-Semitism found in T.S. Eliot and Ezra Pound. In the twenties this attitude was so prevalent that it was an unremarkable, almost unconscious response. Jake Barnes, in fact, bends over backward to be nice to Cohn—almost reverse discrimination. At Scribners, Max Perkins would not let Hemingway use the word "balls," but he did not blink at the word "kike." But to fault Hemingway for his prejudice is to read the novel anachronistically. In 1926 none of the reviewers remarked on Hemingway's treatment of Robert Cohn; his behavior was just what they expected from a rich New York Jew who did not know his place. The novel's anti-Semitism tells us little about its author but a good deal about America in 1926. To forget how we were in the twenties is to read the novel out of context.

"THE BULLS HAVE NO BALLS"

If we forget, for example, just how schizophrenic American moral behavior became in the twenties, we do not fully understand the same curious moral division in *The Sun*. Henry Adams was barely moldering before his prediction that there would never be an American Venus went as flat as the silver screen on which she appeared. Hollywood gave American girls a new role model—the vamp—whose style infected shop girls in Des Moines and kid sisters in Topeka. Corsets disappeared, skirts flapped above the knees, stockings rolled, and one-piece bathing suits clung revealingly to America's daring daughters. The first generation to learn about sexual relationships from the movies began to alienate their parents. When their children embraced Negro jazz music, the parents, for whom the foxtrot was daring and the tango salacious, despaired.

Violent action, in moral Newtonian terms, produced a violent reaction. The Seventh Day Adventists predicted the imminent end of the world; the beast of the apocalypse was upon them. Fundamentalist religions moaned and multiplied; Billy Sunday, sliding in the aisles, led the moral revival with typical American showmanship. Cardinal Hayes pleaded with America to return to God:

> The claim of a new personal freedom—to do as one wants, unrestrained by standards of right and wrong—cannot fail to produce an unhealthy reaction in society. . . . Naked, brutish realism, with a boldness hitherto unknown, challenges from the very housetops, and the distinction of what is clean or unclean, healthy or putrid in literature, art, drama, and public exhibitions is fast being lost sight of. *(Tribune,* January 5, 1925)

While its younger generation went temporarily crazy, the American moral majority frantically tightened the loose screws of the moral locks. Joyce's *Ulysses* was banned from import just when the new American writers most needed it.

Local governments created a plethora of censorship laws to keep virginal minds pure. Publishers walked in fear of censorship. Scribners would not let Mike Campbell say "The bulls have no balls," for they were sure that word alone would doom the book. Under pressure, Hemingway changed it to "The bulls have no horns." In the *Tribune,* Mencken fumed about the Clean Books Bill. "The aim of this bill," he said, "is to make it impossible for a publisher accused of publishing an immoral book to make any defense at all" (January 11, 1925).

Not even Paris, which home-bound Americans knew to be Sin City, was exempt from the reformers, who exported their zeal, along with the Rotary Club, to France. They tried in 1925 to clean up the nightclub acts, which were filled with American show girls playing mostly to tourist audiences. They failed. On January 8, 1925, "The pretty Hoffman girls performing 'Black Mass' in Montmartre were cleared of charges of indecency filed by 'reformers'" (*Tribune*). That was the year that Harry Pilcer put bare-breasted feather dancers into his Acacia Club and Josephine Baker, black, beautiful, and very bare, lit up the Paris night in the Revue Negre. Parisians might not approve of all that jazz, but they were not going to let American prudery dictate their entertainment any more than they were going to allow the Prohibition movement to gain a foothold in Gaul.

Prohibition, of course, was the most obvious example of the insane division in the American moral fabric. By 1925 the *New Republic,* the *American Mercury,* and most of the newspapers were reporting a continuing dialogue between those who were certain that Prohibition was a ridiculous failure and their moral opponents who argued that it was working. That spring the U.S. Navy and Coast Guard sent out an armed flotilla to prevent organized rum runners from landing on the East Coast. The results were as mixed as the cocktails that half of America consumed and that the *Mercury* called an American art form. In Congress, the drinkers kept trying to take the edge off Prohibition without alienating the voters back home. Moral opponents turned back their every effort. . . .

BRETT RINGS IN THE NEW AGE

Our time is not *The Sun's* time. Today Brett Ashley, with her liberated attitudes, seems our contemporary; in the twenties she was not the norm, but the new wave. In 1925 she was on the leading edge of the sexual revolution that produced two types of the "new woman": the educated professional woman who was active in formerly all-male areas and the stylish, uninhibited young woman who drank and smoked in public, devalued sexual innocence, married but did not want children, and considered divorce no social stigma. The first type met with sometimes hysterical resistance from male America. Emma Goldman, radical political activist, was deported. Ma Ferguson, elected governor of Texas, faced rabid male chauvinism in the national press. The *American Mercury*, so critical of the country's cultural wasteland, still felt that woman's place was in the home:

> As soon as a woman steps into the male motley, her dignity begins to vanish.... She idiotically assumes that a day of feminism has arrived—that it is time to cast off certain "shackles" and take her place beside man, the heroic. . . . Well, it simply won't work.

The so-called ladies' magazines did little to promote economic or political independence for women. Edited by men, they continued to portray women in ads, features, and fiction as nest builders. The movies, on the other hand, turned women into sexual objects, churning out films like *The Hell Cat, The She Devil, The Scarlet Woman, The Sin Woman, The Scarlet Sin, The Mortal Sin,* and *Sins of Mothers.* The American male in the twenties could accept woman as either mother or vamp, but not as his economic equal.

Quite obviously Brett Ashley is not a new woman competing in the male marketplace. She is, rather, Hemingway's sophisticated version of the screen vamp. The scene in Pamplona when, wreathed with garlic in the cellar bar, she is surrounded by male dancers could have come from a number of Hollywood films. Twice divorced, Brett has a child she seldom sees; engaged to Mike Campbell, she has seemingly inconsequential affairs with Cohn and Romero that leave her without feelings of guilt or remorse. Brett's rather blasé attitude toward divorce seems today thoroughly modern. In 1926 it was a sign of the times. In 1923 the U.S. divorce rate soared; 165,226 American couples split up that year. For the next several years the figure continued to climb.

The "quickie" divorce was all the rage, and Paris was its center: the divorce mill of Europe. Sparrow Robertson's ad in the Paris *Tribune* was symptomatic of the era: "My wife having left my bed and board I will not be responsible for any bills run up at Kileys, 25 Rue Fontaine, Montmartre" (January 1, 1925). Perhaps because it was more newsworthy, the newspaper emphasized the women who were divorcing their husbands. In 1925, scarcely a week went by without a front-page *Tribune* story of American women granted a Paris divorce.

GLORIA SWANSON GETS PARIS DIVORCE

(Jan. 9)

FOUR AMERICAN WOMEN IN PARIS GET DIVORCES

(Apr. 24)

MAE MURRY, FILM STAR, IS DIVORCED

(May 27)

Only the rich or famous made the paper. Hundreds of other American women divorced that year in Paris without much fanfare.

THE SUN ALSO SETS

In 1927 Hemingway's marriage to Hadley Richardson became one more number in the growing divorce figure. Although Hemingway himself would divorce three wives, he never did it with ease, always forcing his wife to make the decision. His Oak Park values never allowed him to divorce lightly or without remorse, particularly remorse for leaving Hadley. One subtext for *The Sun Also Rises* is the Hemingway marriage, which was coming apart as Hemingway revised his manuscript. He dedicated the novel to Hadley and their son, John; in the divorce settlement, he gave Hadley all of the royalties from *The Sun*. Jake is not Hemingway, but Jake's frustration does epitomize that of his author. Raised in a time when sexual continence, fidelity, and the marriage vows were socially binding, Hemingway found himself in a sexually liberated era that he could not participate in without feeling guilty. The nation's sexual dilemma, which Hemingway understood in his private life, finds its ironic metaphor in Jake Barnes. If ever a man was strapped into a moral straightjacket, it is Jake: impotent and impossibly in love with Brett. . . .

Jake's final condition frequently escapes the contemporary reader, who lacks the historical context for reading the novel. If one misses the ironic and understated references, it may not seem like "such a hell of a sad story" as it did to

Hemingway. Unless one understands the moral background of the period, one may find the Latin Quarter life nostalgically romantic and fail to see the reflection of America self-destructing in the twenties. The blithe reader may see Cohn as the cause of all the troubles. It was not Cohn; it was the times. It was Jake Barnes, impotent in more ways than one, caught in his times, his value system jerked from beneath his feet. He is, finally, the prewar man stripped of all defenses, bereft of values, seduced and abandoned by his times. If at Botin's he gets a bit drunk listening to Brett, perhaps we can forgive him, for both the reader and Jake realize that he is a most ineffectual man in a most unpromising place.

CHAPTER 4

Hemingway's Style in *The Sun Also Rises*

READINGS ON
THE SUN ALSO RISES

Hemingway's Writers in *The Sun Also Rises*

Robert E. Fleming

Hemingway was already highly opinionated on the subject of what made good writing as well as a good writer when he was composing his first novel. In this excerpt from his book on Hemingway's literary alter egos, *The Face in the Mirror*, Robert E. Fleming shows how, using Jake and Cohn as his tortured mouthpieces, Hemingway evaluated the virtues and perils of the writer's life and how *The Sun Also Rises* reflects the balancing act between artistry and commerce. Robert E. Fleming is associate dean of arts and sciences at the University of New Mexico. His other works include *Willard Motley* (1978) and *Sinclair Lewis: A Reference Guide* (1980).

In writing his first novel, Hemingway was torn by his ambivalent attitude about writers and writing. In spite of his own desire to become a successful author, his exposure to the literati of the Left Bank strongly suggested that writers were often self-centered, self-important, and artificial to the point of stifling their own humanity. Such writers were interested only in the impression they would make on others, not on the honesty of their work. A few years later, Hemingway would emphasize the idea of the paramount importance of a writer's honesty and his quest for the truth in nonfiction in his "Monologue to the Maestro," a column written for *Esquire*, where his persona tells an aspiring writer "Good writing is true writing," and at the beginning of *Death in the Afternoon*, where he describes his earliest effort to know "what you really felt, rather than what you were supposed to feel, and had been taught to feel" and to "put down what really happened in action."

In warming up for the writing of *The Sun Also Rises*,

Excerpted from *The Face in the Mirror: Hemingway's Writers*, by Robert E. Fleming. Copyright © 1994 The University of Alabama Press. Reprinted by permission of The University of Alabama Press.

therefore, Hemingway created a narrator much like himself at the time. Jake Barnes is and is not a writer, since he is a reporter rather than a writer of literature and thus corresponds to the reporter facet of Hemingway's own identity in the middle of the 1920s. He can see the literary world from the privileged position of a quasi insider, yet he possesses the perspective to allow him to judge the Paris literary scene and its inhabitants accurately, if sometimes harshly. Unlike the self-conscious literary people who inhabit the Left Bank world, Jake is a journalist who daily goes to his office and files his cables, although for outsiders he maintains a pose: "in the newspaper business . . . it is such an important part of the ethics that you should never seem to be working." Jake's deliberate understatement is an ironic reversal of the expatriate writers' overstatement of their accomplishments: they identify themselves as writers, but they spend their time talking about their work rather than doing it.

JAKE BARNES ON WRITING

In chapter 2 of the original opening of the typescript Hemingway sent to Scribner's, later cut from the galleys of the novel after a suggestion by Scott Fitzgerald, Jake Barnes introduces himself as a newspaper man with certain literary ambitions. After reporting for the New York *Mail* immediately after the war, he went to work, and now works as European director of a news service he helped to found, the Continental Press Association, writing daily dispatches as well as managing the Paris office of the company. He observes the would-be artists of the Quarter with a great deal of scorn, noting that in the Quarter, the "state of mind is principally contempt. Those who work have the greatest contempt for those who don't. The loafers are leading their own lives and it is bad form to mention work. . . . There are contemptuous critics and contemptuous writers. Everybody seems to dislike everybody else." Before he got involved with Brett, Mike, and Robert Cohn, Jake says, he had seldom been in the Quarter except for occasional visits to view the curiosities there.

Jake's explicit meditations on his own feelings about writers and their milieu, wisely excised from the novel at the proofreading stage, may have been a necessary part of Hemingway's own preparation not only for the writing of a novel and the creation of Jake's character but also as an exercise in defining himself as a writer. After several years of working as a journalist and publishing an occasional short story, Hemingway had recently published a real hardcover book with a major American publisher. Now he was beginning a novel that would consolidate his reputation as a serious author. He needed the self-reflective pages at the beginning of the manuscript to help him to understand and construct his own persona as a writer, even though the book was better without them. (He would, incidentally, also write a similar exercise after completion of the novel. Item 530 in the Hemingway collection is a sketch in which Jake Barnes encounters Brett and Mike in the Dingo Bar and attempts to reassure himself that he has done no lasting harm to Brett by publishing his novel.)

Jake's reflections in the first three galleys mirror the quandary in which Hemingway found himself. In spite of his distrust for the literary set and his feeling that he has nothing in common with them, Jake has begun a novel, perhaps because "like all newspaper men I have always wanted to write a novel," even though he realizes that the book may "have that awful taking-the-pen-in-hand quality that afflicts newspaper men when they start to write on their own hook." Jake's fears are, in fact, borne out in the early galleys. He refers to himself quite self-consciously when he explains to the reader that he had planned to write a book in the more objective third person (which would be more consistent with the reporting instincts of a veteran journalist) but that he was forced into the use of the first person by his closeness to Brett Ashley. Because he is so close to the principals, he might have chosen not to write about incidents that will reflect badly on most of them. Why does Jake choose to share his text with an audience? He assures the reader that his motivation is not moral but literary: he is writing his novel solely because he thinks that "it is a good story." Frequently his comments on the Quarter seem self-consciously witty in an artificial literary manner, as Fitzgerald observed when he criticized this version of the opening of the novel. Hemingway, who had already learned the secret of constructing powerful short stories, was working to develop a voice that would sustain interest and sympathy throughout a longer work. . . .

COHN THE POSEUR

Robert Cohn . . . embodies all that is wrong with the writer who is not true to his vocation. If Hemingway began his literary career attempting to know "truly what you really felt, rather than what you were supposed to feel, and had been taught to feel," Cohn spends his time parroting the lessons he has been taught about how he should feel. Unlike Hemingway, who had dedicated himself to his writing since 1919, Cohn has drifted into authorship by accident after his graduation from Princeton. After helping him to squander most of his inheritance, his wife had left him for an artist, so it was only logical that Cohn should try to become an artist of sorts himself. He got his chance on the West Coast, where he "fell among literary people" in Carmel, California. Members of the literary community there persuaded Cohn to use some of the remainder of his inherited money to finance a review of the arts, first as a silent partner and later, when Cohn began to assert himself, as editor. The review later moves to Provincetown, Massachusetts. At odds with the American literary establishment, Hemingway includes a brief slur on the two coastal centers of what he might have regarded as precious literary movements, although the western site produced at least one major poet, Robinson Jeffers, and the eastern location America's major dramatist, Eugene O'Neill.

Cohn's rise from a mere name on the masthead to sole editor of the magazine is explained in purely monetary terms: "It was his money and he discovered he liked the authority of editing." Hemingway's jaundiced view of editors in 1925, gained from a series of what he considered capricious rejections and reinforced by his observations of Ford's editing of the *transatlantic review,* emerges clearly in this part of Cohn's biography. Cohn's review, like many of the little magazines of the 1920s, died after its move to the East Coast, but it died simply because Cohn decided that it had become too expensive. Editors might maintain that they operated their publications for the good of Literature, but decisions were made on the basis of crass financial considerations in the end.

Like a Jamesian character, Cohn continues his eastward pilgrimage—at the prodding of his mistress, Frances Clyne—and eventually settles in Paris. Having dabbled in the arts long enough to become acclimated, Cohn "discovered writing." Hemingway worked hard to convey early in this first chapter just what sort of writer Cohn was. In the galleys cut from the beginning of *The Sun Also Rises,* Jake says that Cohn's book was a "first and last novel," that Cohn was the hero, and that it contained a good deal of fantasy. He then damns it with faint praise, saving that "it was not too badly done" and had been published by a New York firm. In the first chapter of the novel as published, the praise is fainter yet: "He wrote a novel, and it was not really such a bad novel as the critics later called it, although it was a very poor novel." In the latter version, Hemingway manages a statement that cuts both ways, against the critics and against the novelist whose work they condemn—probably for all the wrong reasons.

WRITE WHAT YOU'VE LIVED

Already, Cohn had been deftly created as the sort of author for whom Hemingway could have no respect. For Cohn, writing is one of a rich boy's toys, along with women, travel, and tennis. Like Hubert Elliot, he has bought into the game with his inherited capital and has no fund of experience on which to draw. Robert O. Stephens has observed that, in his prefaces to the books of other writers, Hemingway almost always stresses the personal experience that underlies the work itself, whether it is the drawings of John Groth in *Studio: Europe* or the Spanish civil war novel of Gustave Regler, *The Great Crusade*. Whether writing on war, big-game hunting, or deep-sea fishing, the writer should have lived the experiences before attempting to chronicle them. Hemingway applies this rule to fiction as well as to nonfiction.

If Cohn has no experiences to write about, he also has no compelling reasons to write about them, at least no reasons that Hemingway would consider valid. His motivation is external rather than internal. He writes partly because Frances has decided that he should and partly because it seemed the thing to do after living in the company of literary people in Carmel, Provincetown, and Paris. But Cohn lacks any view of the world to impose on his writing and thus lacks an artistic voice of his own with which to express that view. His ideas must be copies of the ideas of others, his voice an echo of other literary voices. Such imitation, as Emerson had warned his generation, is deadly.

This is not to say that Hemingway believed a writer should ignore the work of other writers. While some types of reading were good only to distract one from his own work, Hemingway told the "maestro" that reading was good for a writer because it showed him what he had to beat in the work of the great writers of the past. More significantly, Hemingway believed—almost like T.S. Eliot—that a special bond connects living writers to those of the past and that reading grounds the writer in the literary tradition of which he will become a part. But once the writer knows that tradition, it is time to break new ground. As Hemingway said in his Nobel Prize acceptance speech, the writing of literature would be easy "if it were only necessary to write in another way what has been well written. It is because we have had such great writers in the past that a writer is driven far out past where he can go, out to where no one can help him." Cohn is familiar with the masterpieces of the past but is unable to add to them because of his own lack of experience with real life. In Emersonian terms, he has studied only books, not nature.

THE "SINISTER GUIDE-BOOK"

If Cohn had been a somewhat pleasant nonentity as an aspiring author, publication brings out the worst facets of his character. When he delivered his manuscript in person, "publishers had praised his novel pretty highly and it rather went to his head." At the same time, lion-hunting women in New York took him up, and Cohn began to see himself as a heroic writer in a Byronic vein. Never self-assured with women, he had previously allowed himself to be manipulated by his wife and by Frances; now he is ripe for sexual adventures befitting a published author who lives in an exotic city.

There is only one thing wrong with Cohn's plan. He has no idea how to become the sort of literary hero he aspires to be. Consequently, he looks for the answer in books: in literary biography and in imaginative fiction, specifically in the novels of W.H. Hudson. Hemingway had nothing against Hudson and in fact greatly admired the Englishman's nature writing. Jake, on the other hand, is more cynical. Describing *The Purple Land* and Cohn's reaction to it, Jake suggests that Cohn is celebrating his male menopause by reliving adolescent schoolboy fantasies. Jake sees the book as "sinister" when it is read by a man of a certain age who will accept uncritically the "amorous adventures" of an Englishman in South America. Cohn accepts the novel as a "guide-book," which he assumes to be as accurate and literal as "an R.G. Dun report." The reference to the Dun report once again links Cohn, literature, and money: Cohn knows something about money and should stick to what he knows. Instead, he obstinately insists on pursuing a dream engendered by the reading of fiction.

In an extended conversation soon after the passage on W.H. Hudson, Hemingway plays off Cohn's artificial attitudes against Jake's sensible nature, which is made up of hard-boiled journalistic cynicism tempered with Emersonian insights. Cohn asks Jake to go with him to South America so that Cohn can begin to live his life. Cohn laments that his life is passing him by without his ever having the expe-

HEMINGWAY'S SUN AS TITLE AND METAPHOR

Jake Barnes takes great notice of the sun's passage and intensity throughout the novel. These factors usually reflect how his life is going right then.

Critics of *The Sun Also Rises* have conventionally seen the title as Hemingway's ironic comment on the tension suggested by the inscriptions from Ecclesiastes I: 4–7 and Gertrude Stein's statement that "You are all a lost generation." Hemingway did not help matters any when he commented in *A Moveable Feast* that he had "tried to balance Miss Stein's quotation from the garage keeper with one from Ecclesiastes," implying that one quotation would in some way offset the other within the events of the novel. "But the hell with her lost-generation talk," he added, "and all the dirty, easy labels," implying once again that he did not believe his generation was any more lost than any other generation.

If extended into the novel, the title and Hemingway's comment may be seen as forming a metaphorical connection between the characters and the events. As Jake, Brett, Mike, Bill, and Cohn pursue a round of meaningless activity day after day, the sun simultaneously rises and sets "and hasteth to the place where he arose." As the characters group and regroup, the sun continues to follow them in a repetitive cycle of entropic, formulaic ritual in Paris and Pamplona, to which Jake is obsessively drawn by the ritual of the bullfights. Hemingway underscored this cycle by opening Chapters five, ten, eleven, and twelve with specific comments on the sun. Chapter Five begins with "It was a fine morning. . . . There was the pleasant early-morning feeling of a hot day," while in Chapter Ten Jake says, "In the morning it was bright" and "Already, so early in the morning, it was very hot. . . ." In Chapter Eleven he com-

riences a writer should have. By his calculations, half of his life has passed, and he has yet to feel really alive. His solution is to seek a storybook land where he can live a storybook life—recreating the adventures he has read in the Hudson novel. Experiences for Cohn can come only through books, not directly from life.

Although ironically Jake too has done his share of running away from problems and will do more in the course of *The Sun Also Rises,* he answers, echoing Emerson, that "going to another country doesn't make any difference. . . . You can't get away from yourself by moving from one place to

---

pulsively comments that "It was baking hot in the square" and "the women all had their fans going in the sun. It certainly was hot." But on the train to Bayonne, conversely, Jake's day had ended as "we passed through the Landes and watched the sun set." Chapter Twelve opens with his comment that "When I woke in the morning I went to the window and looked out. It had cleared and there were no clouds on the mountains." Through the simple expedient of having Jake comment on the sun making everything hot, Hemingway unobtrusively establishes the correlation between the title, the sun, the events, and the characters.

At Pamplona, Jake goes into a church to pray and when he comes out "The sunlight was hot and hard." Even on the bus trip to Roncevaux, he obsessively notes that after a stop "we all went out into the sunlight and the heat, and climbed back on top of the bus." By Chapter Fifteen, however, things are going badly and are reflected in Jake's daily weather report: "In the morning it was raining. A fog had come over the mountains from the sea," but on the last page of the novel—after Jake and Brett are reunited—he says, "It was hot and bright." As suggested by the above passages, Hemingway's use of the title serves to reinforce the thematic pattern of the sun's predictable course by contrasting the unpredictable course of human nature and the pointless circularity of the lives of the characters. Far more than a "balance" between Ecclesiastes and Gertrude Stein's comment, the sun of the title both rises and sets as a metaphorical measurement of the hours in between the days when "One generation passeth away and another generation cometh."

Robert A. Martin, *Hemingway Review,* vol. 6, no. 1, Fall 1986.

another" and observes that Cohn is already living in one of
the most glamorous cities in the world. He suggests that
Cohn begin to live his life in Paris. He should relax, "cruise
around," and simply let life come to him. Experience is necessary for a writer, but Jake has found that experience need
not be sought out if one is active enough. Jake enunciates
the same philosophy of experience that Hemingway would
explain in his introduction to *The First 49:*

> In going where you have to go, and doing what you have to
> do, and seeing what you have to see, you dull and blunt the
> instrument you write with. But I would rather have it bent
> and dull and know I had to put it on the grindstone again and
> hammer it into shape and put a whetstone to it, and know
> that I had something to write about, than to have it bright and
> shining and nothing to say, or smooth and well-oiled in the
> closet, but unused.

Cohn's "instrument" has remained unused throughout his
life. He has unsuccessfully tried to gain experience, but his
effort ended prosaically: he was stopped by a bicycle policeman. Jake gives up the argument, underscoring the problem
with Cohn by remarking that, since Cohn has gotten the idea
that he wants to go to South America from a book, probably
his disillusionment with Paris also comes from a book.

A CENTURY BEHIND THE TIMES

Throughout chapter 2, the main theme is Cohn's bookishness. Rather than live life and then translate his experiences
into literature, Cohn tries to make his life conform to literature. His writing then will be twice removed from reality as
he attempts to emulate the descriptions of life that he finds
in the literature of the past. Moreover, even his sources are
suspect. Like Howells's Editha Balcomb, Cohn is addicted to
romantic literature, and he has to strain to see life in the
terms in which his literary models have presented it. This
characterization is important, for Cohn's predilection to
model his life on literary ideas becomes more pronounced
in later chapters of *The Sun Also Rises.*

In chapter 5, for example, Cohn publicly overreacts when
Jake jokingly tells him to go to hell. More angry than is jus-
tifiable, given the situation, Cohn stands up at their table, his
face white (in comic contrast to the plates of hors d'oeuvres),
while Jake admonishes him to "cut out the prep-school
stuff." Cohn refuses to sit down again until Jake has taken
back his remark. If this episode smacks of prep school, so

does the incident that sparks the argument, for Cohn has been romantically defending the honor of Brett Ashley: he had asked Jake to tell him what he knows of Brett but is then offended by Jake's frank cynicism.

In chapter 6 Cohn's immaturity is underscored when Harvey Stone sums up his character. Harvey pays him the mock compliment of telling Cohn that he is not a moron but then says, "You're only a case of arrested development." Cohn is a case of arrested development in a literary sense as well as in the personal sense of having the emotional development of an adolescent: while in the midst of a hotbed of avant-garde literary movements, he imitates century-old literary attitudes. When his lady fair is attacked, he prepares to invoke the code duello more appropriate to the 1820s than to the 1920s. . . .

THE NOBLE TALE OF SIR COHN

Nowhere is Cohn's bookishness more apparent than in his dealings with Brett Ashley. After they have lived together at San Sebastian, Cohn refuses to call off his trip to Spain with Jake, Brett, and Brett's fiancé, Mike Campbell. Jake is puzzled about Cohn's willingness to put himself in such an embarrassing position, but when an argument breaks out in a Pamplona café, something about Cohn's look gives Jake the insight to explain Cohn's behavior. He realizes that Robert has put up with the agony of seeing Brett with another man and has suffered the insults that Mike and others have heaped on him because "it was his affair with a lady of title." Once again Cohn's attention is less on the pain of the current situation than on how the events might look to a hypothetical literary biographer. A painful affair with "a lady of title" is enriched when things do not go smoothly. If Cohn cannot bring himself to use the Pamplona incidents in a future novel, at least they will linger in his memory as actions appropriate to the life of a literary gentleman. When Mike threatens Robert physically, he stands proudly and happily, "ready to do battle for his lady love."

Although no battle materializes on this occasion, Cohn has an opportunity to act out yet another romantic cliché later, when Brett falls in love with Pedro Romero, the young matador. Cohn attempts to save Brett from the bullfighter by going to the matador's room while Brett is there, planning to "make an honest woman of her." Instead, he gets into a fight with Romero, whom he repeatedly knocks to the floor. In spite of his superior boxing skills, Cohn is unable to defeat Romero, however, for Romero refuses to acknowledge that he has been beaten. Cohn's romantic attitudes have at last encountered a reality that they cannot overcome. Brett refuses to leave Romero's room with Cohn, Romero remains spiritually undefeated, and both refuse to reconcile with Robert Cohn on his schoolboy terms—by shaking hands with him as if they were all characters in a juvenile novel. Cohn leaves Pamplona the next day, completely "ruined," as Mike says. He can no longer maintain the role of swash-buckling writer that he has conceived for himself.

Of course, not every writer appearing in *The Sun Also Rises* is satirized. Jake's close friend Bill Gorton, for example, is treated sympathetically and furnishes some of the most amusing lines in the novel, often making jokes at his own expense, as Robert would never do. In clear contrast to Cohn, Gorton embraces life's experiences and recognizes the primacy of life over art. Juxtaposed with a matador who faces death every time he enters the ring, Bill admittedly feels inferior to the man of action.

VANITY IN VAIN

While Hemingway's treatment of writers and writing is not the main theme of his first novel, it nevertheless supports that theme and continues to develop Hemingway's evolving philosophy. During the 1920s Hemingway had been modifying and enlarging his notion of what a writer could and should be, and the book documents his formation of strong opinions on the subject, primarily by negative definition. Most of the writers who appear in the novel—Prentiss, Braddocks, and Cohn—are treated as artificial, lacking in sincere, deep emotions, and less perceptive than the average person rather than more so. All of the full-time writers except Bill Gorton also lack joy in their lives; they seem unable to laugh, especially at themselves. In keeping with the second epigraph of the novel, Cohn, at least, is obsessed with the vanity of his own literary ambitions, often to such a degree that he cannot correctly interpret what is happening in the real world. The vanity of the writer, then, is set in the larger context of mankind's vanity, which Hemingway (like the preacher of Ecclesiastes) has been attacking. Against the permanence of sun and wind, rivers and sea, humankind seems small and insignificant.

The Sun Also Rises serves as Hemingway's first major evaluation of the role of the writer. While the novel only hints at a more sinister side of the writer that would be exposed in the stories and novels of the 1930s, it significantly betrays the fact that even the young Hemingway harbored deep misgivings about whether a writer could balance his personal life and his professional life, whether it was morally proper to use one's own life and the lives of one's friends and family as literary material, and whether a writer could withstand the notoriety that comes with success. The novel foreshadows psychological conflicts of which Hemingway himself might not yet have been conscious.

Humor in *The Sun Also Rises*

James Hinkle

Few critics have praised *The Sun Also Rises* as humorous, yet James Hinkle's careful survey of the text yields a surprising number of embedded quips, barbs, and double entendres. No other novel by Hemingway is so filled to bursting with craftily submerged seeds of wordplay. James Hinkle is the author of *Reading Faulkner: The Unvanquished.*

"Hemingway, why do you always come here drunk?"

"I don't know, Miss Stein, unless it's to see you." (quoted in John Atkins, *The Art of Ernest Hemingway*)

"Uh, it was a joke then."

"Yes. To laugh at." (*The Sun Also Rises*)

Readers have come up with many reasons for admiring *The Sun Also Rises* but no one, so far as I know, has made much of the jokes in the novel. The free-associating banter of Bill Gorton, the fractured English of Count Mippipopolous, occasional sardonic comments by the narrator, Jake Barnes, have of course been noted. But jokes in *The Sun Also Rises?* What jokes? Most readers seem to find the book no funnier than did Harold Loeb, prototype of *The Sun Also Rises*'s humorless Robert Cohn: "I do not remember that Hem was much of a spoofer as a young man. Perhaps he developed a taste for it as age overtook him." The prototype of Bill Gorton, Donald Ogden Stewart, a professional humorist himself, said flatly that "written humor was not his [Hemingway's] dish."

Yet I propose to point to [dozens of] submerged jokes in *The Sun Also Rises*—if by "jokes" I can be understood to mean all of the various kinds of plays on words whose effect is incongruous or funny once they are recognized. Few of them will make anyone roll in the aisle, but they have their

Excerpted from "What's Funny in *The Sun Also Rises*," by James Hinkle, *The Hemingway Review*, vol. 4, no. 2, pp. 31–41. Reprinted by permission of *The Hemingway Review.*

moments. My aim is not to defend Hemingway's sense of humor or to sort his jokes into categories. My aim is simply to identify his jokes—to demonstrate by example that there are many more of them in *The Sun Also Rises* than we have realized. Playing with the multiple meanings inherent in words is a pervasive feature of Hemingway's writing.

Most readers have approached Hemingway with serious expectations, and these expectations have determined pretty much and limited what they have found. But Hemingway always claimed to be at least a part-time humorist. He is consistently unsympathetic to those who looked down on him when he himself "committed levity":

> [L]ots of criticism is written by characters who are very academic and think it is a sign you are worthless if you make jokes or kid or even clown.

> The bastards don't want you to joke because it disturbs their categories.

> "Joke people and you make enemies. That's what I always say."

Anyone who has read through Hemingway's letters must have been struck by his persistent reliance on humor. Even when he is most serious he often develops his argument in an ironic or flippant or mocking tone. We know from his letters that he thought the first draft of *The Sun Also Rises* was funny. *The Torrents of Spring,* clearly intended as a funny performance, he wrote between finishing the *The Sun Also Rises* first draft and before starting the revision. And in an inscribed copy of the printed *The Sun Also Rises* Hemingway called the novel a "little treatise on promiscuity including a Few Jokes."

I want to present my . . . *The Sun Also Rises* jokes roughly in order of their difficulty, moving from relatively obvious examples to more subtle or ingenious or likely-to-be-overlooked ones. Begin with a simple pun whose effect is mild humor:

> Everything is on such a clear financial basis in France. . . . If you want people to like you you have only to spend a little money. I spent a little money and the waiter liked me. He appreciated my valuable qualities.

But that is not a typical *The Sun Also Rises* pun, because it calls attention to itself. Most of Hemingway's puns are less insistent:

> Brett was radiant. . . . The sun was out and the day was bright.

That should be a clear example. Here is another:

for six months I never slept with the electric light off. That was another bright idea.

Sometimes a pun is introduced and then played with:

The publishers had praised his [Cohn's] novel pretty highly and it rather went to his head.

Where else except up would high praise go? This is followed on the next page by adding "steep" to the pun on "high":

playing for higher stakes than he could afford in some rather steep bridge games.

Another example:

In the dark I could not see his face very well.

"Well," I said, "see you in the morning."

That is a variation of:

There is no reason why because it is dark you should look at things differently from when it is light. The hell there isn't!

TRIPLE ENTENDRES AND BACKHANDED LOBS

The narrator, Jake Barnes, is not the only one in the book who is alive to puns. On the evening Bill Gorton arrives in Paris Jake asks him:

"What'll we do to-night?"

"Doesn't make any difference. Only let's not get daunted. Suppose they got any hard-boiled eggs here?"

"Hard-boiled" eggs to guard against becoming daunted. The meaning of "hard-boiled" we already know from Jake:

It is awfully easy to be hard-boiled about everything in the daytime, but at night it is another thing.

Sometimes the pun depends on the reader knowing at least something of a foreign language. After Cohn and Jake have their first near-fight:

we walked up to the Café de la Paix and had coffee.

At least one *The Sun Also Rises* pun is based on a catch-phrase of the day. When Jake leaves Cohn at the end of the first chapter he says:

"I'll see you to-morrow at the courts."

He means the tennis courts, but his sentence is a play on "See you in court."

Sometimes *The Sun Also Rises*'s words make a statement that is literally true in more ways than the presumably in-tended one. While the effect of these second meanings is usually funny, that is not always the case. Consider the scene when Jake learns from Brett that it was Robert Cohn she had gone to San Sebastian with:

"Who did you think I went down to San Sebastian with?"

"Congratulations," I said. . . .

We walked along and turned a corner.

Their relationship at that moment did indeed turn a corner. Jake can't keep back his bitterness after Brett explains that she rather thought the experience would be good for Cohn:

"You might take up social service."

"Don't be nasty."

Shortly after Jake has helped set up Brett with Romero, Cohn comes looking for her:

"Where's Brett?" he asked.

"I don't know."

"She was with you."

"She must have gone to bed."

Yes, that is exactly where she is—in bed, with Romero.

When Brett and Jake approach the Café Select after reaching a romantic impasse in a Paris cab:

On the Boulevard Raspail, with the lights of Montparnasse in sight, Brett said:

"Would you mind very much if I asked you to do something?"

"Don't be silly."

"Kiss me just once more before we get there."

When the taxi stopped I got out and paid.

That last is quite a line. Literally it means that Jake gives the taxi driver five or ten francs. But it also means that Jake has an emotional price to pay for his hour in the cab close to Brett. He leaves the Select shortly afterward, walks to his apartment alone, thinks of his wound and of Brett, and then cries himself to sleep.

Mike sees that Brett has a new hat:

"Where did you get that hat?"

"Chap bought it for me. Don't you like it?"

Doesn't he like what? The hat or the idea that a man bought it for her? The first is probably what Brett intended but the second has more meaning for the novel.

Brett makes a remark to Romero that the reader can (and probably should) take in more than one way:

"The bulls are my best friends. . . ."

"You kill your friends?" she asked.

"Always," he said in English, and laughed. "So they don't kill me." He looked at her across the table.

"You know English well."

There are three meanings in Brett's last comment: first, she could be simply complimenting Romero on his ability to speak English; second, she could be saying that his sure manner, his way of looking at her, show that he knows very well how to make himself attractive to a English lady; third, and more ominous, she could be saying that he knows English people very well if he realizes that English friends could kill him. This last meaning is supported by several other passages: Mike says it was his friends, false friends, that did him in. Montoya says about Romero: "Any foreigner can flatter him. They start this Grand Hotel business, and in one year they're through." Jake has already told us that "any foreigner was an Englishman," and Brett says in Madrid after she had sent Romero away, "I'd have lived with him if I hadn't seen it was bad for him," and she hopes it is true when she says "I don't think I hurt him any."

THROWAWAY RELIGIOUS HUMOR

Religion is put in its place by one brief comment:

That afternoon was the big religious procession. San Fermin was translated from one church to another. . . .

"Isn't that the procession?" Mike asked.

"Nada," some one said. "It's nothing."

Jake goes to confession several times in Pamplona. Brett would like to go with him but Jake tells her:

not only was it impossible but it was not as interesting as it sounded, and, besides, it would be in a language she did not know.

Jake's minor joke here is that his confession would not be likely to interest Brett because he does not have any sexual items to report. A more significant meaning concerns the language Brett would not understand. Confessions in a Spanish church would be in Spanish. But in the following sentence we learn that Brett has her fortune told at a gypsy camp, and that too would be in Spanish, and there is no mention then of her not being able to understand what was said. Nor does she have any trouble understanding and being understood by Romero, or the other Spanish men who use her as an image to dance around or to sing to in their hard Spanish voices. The point seems to be that it is the language of the church that Brett doesn't know and it makes no difference whether one takes that to be Spanish or Latin. As she says herself, "I'm damn bad for a religious atmosphere. I've the wrong type of face."

At the end of the book Brett suggests that the satisfaction resulting from decent behavior might substitute for the consolation of religion. Jake is not so sure, so he gently proposes a pain-killer more in line with her temperament:

> "You know it makes one feel rather good deciding not to be a bitch. . . . It's sort of what we have instead of God." . . .

A WORD IS A WORD IS A WORD

Words deliberately taken as words are the basis of much of the humor in *The Sun Also Rises*. The simplest form of this basic joke in *The Sun Also Rises* can be seen when Jake tries to get by difficult moments with Brett by responding literally to her words rather than to their intended meaning:

> "Don't look like that, darling."
>
> "How do you want me to look?"
>
> "What did you say that for?"
>
> "I don't know. What would you like me to say?"
>
> "Darling, don't let's talk a lot of rot."
>
> "All right. Talk about anything you like."
>
> "I was in school in Paris, then. Think of that."
>
> "Anything you want me to think about it?"

Sometimes the literal joke is buried in a seemingly innocent remark. After Cohn knocks Jake out, Jake reluctantly goes to Cohn's room and finds Cohn feeling sorry for himself:

> "Now everything's gone. Everything."
>
> "Well," I said, "so long. I've got to go."

and:

> "You were the only friend I had."
>
> "Well," I said, "so long."

One time Cohn drops by Jake's Paris office and wants to talk. When it becomes apparent Cohn isn't going to leave, Jake invites him downstairs for a drink:

"Aren't you working?"

"No," I said.

Literally that is an accurate response. Jake isn't working; he is at the moment talking with Cohn. But he wants to work and is maneuvering to get rid of Cohn so he can get back to work.

"Hell" is the subject of several instances of unexpected literalness. In one, Jake has just told Cohn that Brett is a drunk and is going to marry Mike Campbell:

"I don't believe it." . . .

"You asked me what I knew about Brett Ashley."

"I didn't ask you to insult her."

"Oh, go to hell."

He stood up from the table his face white, and stood there white and angry behind the little plates of hors d'oeuvres.

"Sit down," I said. "Don't be a fool."

"You've got to take that back."

"Oh, cut out the prep-school stuff."

"Take it back."

"Sure. Anything. I never heard of Brett Ashley. How's that?"

"No. Not that. About me going to hell."

"Oh, don't go to hell," I said. "Stick around. We're just starting lunch."

Jake suggests the crowded condition of hell when he is talking with Cohn about going to South America:

"Well, why don't you start off?"

"Frances."

"Well," I said, "take her with you."

"She wouldn't like it. That isn't the sort of thing she likes. She likes a lot of people around."

"Tell her to go to hell."

An interesting use of hell occurs after Jake has helped set up Brett with Romero and then Cohn comes looking for her:

"Tell me where Brett is."

"I'll not tell you a damn thing."

"You know where she is."

"If I did I wouldn't tell you."

"Oh, go to hell, Cohn," Mike called from the table. "Brett's gone off with the bull-fighter chap. They're on their honeymoon."

"You shut up."

"Oh go to hell!" Mike said languidly.

"Is that where she is?" Cohn turned to me.

"Go to hell!"

"She was with you. Is that where she is?"

"Go to hell!"

It is hard to say whether Cohn's "Is that where she is?" refers primarily to "honeymoon" or "hell"—if the two are not indeed the same thing, for when Jake gets to Madrid to rescue Brett from her "honeymoon" she reports: "I've had such a hell of a time," and earlier she had said about being in love: "I think it's hell on earth." . . .

THE FIRST WORD THAT COMES INTO YOUR HEAD

Sometimes words trigger a bizarre train of thought. A waiter asks:

"Shrimps?"

"Is Cohn gone?" Brett asked.

Sometimes an expression is acted out:

"Ask her if she's got any jam," Bill said. "Be ironical with her."

"Have you got any jam?"

"That's not ironical.". . .

The girl brought in a glass dish of raspberry jam. . . .

"Poor," said Bill. "Very poor. You can't do it."

Bill and the waitress in different ways give Jake the raspberry.

Brett comes to Jake's room and wakes him up at half-past four in the morning. Jake makes drinks and listens while Brett talks on about her evening with Count Mippipopolous: "Offered me ten thousand dollars to go to Biarritz with him. . . . Told him I knew too many people in Biarritz." Brett laughs but Jake doesn't.

"I say, you are slow on the up-take," she said. I had only sipped my brandy and soda. I took a long drink.

"That's better. Very funny."

Jake's taking a long drink is not simply a clever response to Brett's saying he is "slow on the uptake." It is also his way of indicating he had understood when Brett on the previous page by taking a drink had acted out one meaning for "one of us":

> "The count? Oh, rather. He's quite one of us."

> "Is he a count?"

> "Here's how.". . . She sipped at her glass.

Occasionally a passage needs to be read aloud for us to realize what is funny. Brett first appears in the book at a bal musette with a group of flamboyant male homosexuals. We recognize them by how they talk when they see Georgette:

> "I do declare. There is an actual harlot. I'm going to dance with her, Lett. You watch me."

> The tall dark one, called Lett, said: "Don't you be rash."

> The wavy blond one answered: "Don't you worry, dear." And with them was Brett.

Hemingway and Jake do not care for homosexuals. Jake was away. When he returns to the bal Mrs. Braddocks brings up a young man and introduces him as Robert Prentiss. If we continue reading aloud we discover that Prentiss too must have been part of Brett's entourage:

> He was from New York by way of Chicago, and was a rising new novelist. He had some sort of an English accent. I asked him to have a drink.

> "Thanks so much," he said. "I've just had one."

> "Have another."

> "Thanks, I will then.". . . "You're from Kansas City, they tell me," he said.

> "Yes."

> "Do you find Paris amusing?"

> "Yes."

> "Really?". . .

> "For God's sake," I said, "yes. Don't you?"

> "Oh, how charmingly you get angry," he said. "I wish I had that faculty."

When Jake hears that last speech, he gets up and walks away again. Mrs. Braddocks follows:

"Don't be cross with Robert," she said. "He's still only a child, you know."

"I wasn't cross," I said. "I just thought perhaps I was going to throw up."

Robert Cohn wants to be a writer, but listen to his first words in the book:

"For God's sake, why did you say that about that girl in Strasbourg for?"

Can anyone who can say a sentence like that ever become a decent writer? . . .

THE POLICEMAN'S ENSEMBLE

Near the beginning of the book Jake watches a red and green stop-and-go traffic signal. At the end he sees a traffic policeman raise his baton, forcing the cab Jake is riding in with Brett to a sudden halt. Between these two scenes we find a number of references to people waving things—the drummer waving his drumsticks, Bill waving a chicken drumstick, Marshal Ney waving his sword, "the inventor of the semaphore engaged in doing same." All seem to prepare us for the policeman's raised baton of the final page. It would be hard to imagine a more explicit symbolic acting out of a reminder of the reason Jake cannot satisfy Brett.

I am not the first, of course, to have noticed the sexual overtones of the policeman's raised baton, but I am not aware that anyone has spelled out how the details of the scene work. The baton is a twelve-inch white club. When not being used—when it is at rest—it dangles from the policeman's waist. The policeman is a "mounted" policeman. "Mounted" is itself a sexual word. Presumably here it means that he is riding a horse—thus in the saddle, an easy rider—and this takes us back to Bill's "puts a man on her horse" which is in turn based on "puts lead in your pencil." The policeman is wearing khaki. That suggests a military uniform and is a reminder of the reason Jake cannot now go ahead. But khaki (rhymes with "tacky") is a relatively recent and specifically American pronunciation. In the 1920s in Europe it was "cock-ee" which has an unavoidable sexual suggestion. Add to this that a few minutes earlier Jake had trouble entering Brett's hotel because he could not make "the elevator" work, and then he was told that the personages of her establishment were "rigidly selected." The policeman's raised baton forces Jake to confront the fact that he will never qualify for admission to Brett, since "making the elevator work" and a selection process involving "rigid" represent for him impossible requirements.

Jake's jokes (and thus Hemingway's in *The Sun Also Rises*) are all in the ironic mode—variations on Bill's "Give them Irony and Give them Pity." Surely, taken together, and at the very least, the jokes represent one possible and reasonably effective defensive stance for someone who has been wounded in a rotten way on a joke front—which, less literally, seems to have been the situation of almost all young men and women of feeling after World War I.

The Art of Repetition in *The Sun Also Rises*

E. Miller Budick

E. Miller Budick is the author of *Engendering Romance: Women Writers and the Hawthorne Tradition* and *Emily Dickinson and the Life of Language: A Study in Symbolic Poetics*. He has also written articles on numerous writers including Arthur Miller and Sylvia Plath.
Here Budick shows how Hemingway deliberately repeats description and dialogue throughout the text. These refrains underscore the irony of the characters' shifting moods and how the more frenziedly they try to stay in motion, the more obliviously they come looping back to their original straits.

Hemingway's novel of restatement, in which Hemingway tells the story of Jake Barnes, who tells his own story and the story of Robert Cohn, which is in itself a reformulation of the story of the American dream, suggests that it is only in self-aware repetition—accompanied by the achievement of an inner self-control—that the cycling of human experience becomes more than repressive *déjà vu*. Throughout Hemingway's novel, experiences, statements, characters, and stories double each other with an almost hysteria-inducing regularity. 'I'm so miserable,' Brett whines at regular intervals to the ever-sympathetic Jake. . . . And in perhaps the most terrifying occurrence of dream-like replay, Jake's and Brett's final car ride repeats their first such moment together in the novel (though, as I shall try to show in a moment, with a significant difference). Fishing trips, bullfights, and swimming episodes reincarnate each other, as do scenes and conversations around dining-room tables and in bars. Robert Cohn doubles Jake Barnes, as does Romero later in the book.

But Jake does not see the duplications which his story

Excerpted from "*The Sun Also Rises:* Hemingway and the Art of Repetition," by E. Miller Budick, *University of Toronto Quarterly*, vol. 56, no. 2, pp. 328–35 (1986–1987). Reprinted by permission of University of Toronto Press Incorporated.

records. 'I had that feeling of going through something that has all happened before,' Jake reports early in the novel. 'I had the feeling as in a nightmare of it all being something repeated, something I had been through and that now I must go through again.' Such a moment of *déjà vu* is not self-knowledge and self-reflexive commentary. It is an effort of the mind to forget what it has unconsciously remembered. It is repression, of the kind that characterizes much of Jake's narrative enterprise. Not insignificantly, this moment of repressed awareness of his almost warlike march to the pulsations of Brett's sexual rhythms is accompanied in the text by the meaningless beat of the drummer, whose voiceless hypnotic power is represented in the story by the mechanical sign '. . . . . .' repeated three times. Jake is victim to a drum beat which he is powerless to stop. Indeed, it is reproduced maddeningly in the staccato of his text. He cannot control the nightmarish repetition of experience which is represented in the novel both by the literal re-enactment of events and, even more nightmarishly, by his recastings of his own emotions as the feelings and thoughts of others. Because he has not yet penetrated to meaning and self-knowledge he is a poor interpreter of the nightmare which has become his life and art.

NEITHER JAKE NOR COHN IS A GOOD READER

This problem of psychological and artistic control results, for Hemingway, from an inability to get the text right. From both Jake's and Hemingway's points of view, the wrong kinds of texts are being published. Even more troubling, those who cannot write texts also do not know how to read them:

> [Cohn] had been reading W.H. Hudson. That sounds like an innocent occupation, but Cohn had read and reread 'The Purple Land.' 'The Purple Land' is a very sinister book if read too late in life. It recounts splendid imaginary amorous adventures of a perfect English gentleman in an intensely romantic land, the scenery of which is very well described. For a man to take it at thirty-four as a guide-book to what life holds is about as safe as it would be for a man of the same age to enter Wall Street direct from a French convent, equipped with a complete set of the more practical Alger books. Cohn, I believe, took every word of 'The Purple Land' as literally as though it had been an R.G. Dun report. You understand me, he made some reservations, but on the whole the book to him was sound. It was all that was needed to set him off.

The references here to 'The Purple Land' (alliteratively suggesting the same 'promised land' of which Cohn is also enamoured), and to Wall Street, Horatio Alger, and the French convent, set up allusions which point to the issues, public and private, which circulate in the book as a whole, issues of the American dream, biblical metaphor, and emotional health. More important, the passage specifically links these problems to the matter of textual misinterpretation. Cohn's failure as an interpreter of texts is that he literalistically reads and rereads his 'Bible' and, like an American Puritan now shown for the Jew he really is, believes perversely in the purple, promised land that has, in Christianity, already been superseded. Robert Cohn is the priest (a Hebrew *cohen*—at one point Bill asks what the word 'Cohn' means), or perhaps a 'convent' nun or monk (suggesting some of Hemingway's and Jake's reservations about Cohn's sexuality), who imposes a rigidly spiritual and therefore destructively naive perception of reality upon a complex sexually and emotionally charged universe. Cohn cannot read critically or self-consciously. In the portrait of the 'splendid imaginary amorous adventures of a perfect English gentleman in an intensely romantic land,' he cannot discern a critical reflection of himself.

Though Jake comprehends Cohn's failure as a writer and reader, he does not see that he himself has been a similarly failed reader of texts. His story of Cohn, down to such details as the English-gentleman-like Cohn's amorous adventures and the well-described scenery, is a self-portrait. But Jake does not see himself implicated in what he has read or written:

> It was a little past noon and there was not much shade, but I sat against the trunk of two of the trees that grew together, and read. The book was something by A.E.W. Mason, and I was reading a wonderful story about a man who had been frozen in the Alps and then fallen into a glacier and disappeared, and his bride was going to wait twenty-four years exactly for his body to come out on the moraine, while her true love waited too, and they were still waiting when Bill came up.

Jake gives no evidence that he is aware that the Mason novel symbolically evokes his own situation, though, by having him collapse levels of reference when he says that they, the characters in the Mason story, were still waiting when *Bill* came up, Hemingway signals that the story and the reality are significantly related. But Jake does not understand why he recalls this moment, nor can he use the insights which a self-conscious reading of the novel might have afforded. (Compare Jake's denial of his feeling for Brett and the consequences of that denial later in the same scene.)

ROMERO KEEPS IT REAL

For Hemingway the bullfight is the new testament, the psychologically, spiritually, and artistically potent text of the modern world. Not everyone will be able to understand and accept this new law: 'The Biarritz crowd . . . thought Romero was afraid [and they] preferred Belmonte's imitation of himself or Marcial's imitation of Belmonte.' But it is a text to which Jake can and does respond, and having read, can rewrite, Hemingway-style, in his life and work.

The bullfight completes the process of psychological purging which begins in Romero's fist-fight with Cohn. Psychological health precedes artistic success. But the bullfight is more than psychotherapy. Because Romero is able to integrate his emotions and bring them to bear on the one perfect object, he converts psychological force into artistic, sexual, and religious power. There is no repression here, no fantasy overtaking life:

> Pedro Romero had the greatness. He loved bull-fighting, and I think he loved the bulls, and I think he loved Brett. Everything of which he could control the locality he did in front of her all that afternoon. Never once did he look up. He made it stronger that way, and did it for himself, too, as well as for her. Because he did not look up to ask if it pleased he did it all for himself inside, and it strengthened him, and yet he did it for her, too. But he did not do it for her at any loss to himself.

Romero loves the bull and identifies with it. But he does not mistake the bull for himself. He does not project himself onto it and see himself reflected in it. He remains separate, in control. And just as Romero maintains a purity of perception in relation to the bull, which means, conversely, that he retains an integrity of self, so no distorting 'legend' contaminates his own performance.

Because Romero accepts his basic aggressiveness, he is able to transform it into love. Romero and the bull (and by implication, Brett) are 'one.' They are joined by the phallic 'sword,' which is activated (not immobilized as in the statue of Marshal Ney) in an assault which is as loving as it is violent:

> The bull wanted it again. . . . Each time he let the bull pass so close that the man and the bull . . . were . . . one . . . for an instant he and the bull were one, Romero way out over the bull,

> the right arm extended high up to where the hilt of the sword
> had gone in between the bull's shoulders. Then the figure
> was broken. There was a little jolt as Romero came clear.

Romero uses his sword not only to unite himself with the
bull, but also to protect himself from it. The bullfight acknowledges the violent component of sexuality. It accepts the
life-and-death relationship between lovers. It permits the ho-
mosexual aspects of love, and their dangers and therefore the
necessary resistance to them, even (or especially) in the context of heterosexual love. Hence, the bullfight comes to represent for Hemingway (and for Jake) an image of perfect art,
perfect life, perfect love, and, one must add, perfect religion.

JAKE SEES THE LIGHT UNDERWATER

Not accidentally, the faith which bullfighting expresses is
the faith of *'afición,'* 'passion,' that link between the physical
and the spiritual which has, in Jake, as in America, broken
down. Montoya is the priest of this religion who, Puritan-
like, administers 'a sort of spiritual examination' to potential
adherents and who allows into the church of the elect only
those who can provide a proper expression of this faith. But
unlike the American Puritans and their descendants, Montoya and the other priests of *afición* understand the importance of the physical, so that admission into their church is
always accompanied by an 'embarrassed putting the hand
on the shoulder, or a "Buen hombre" . . . nearly always there
was the actual touching' (the complex, 'embarrassed,' ho-
mosexual potential is again evident). Jake knows the value
of the religion of bullfighting ('Nobody ever lives their life all
the way up except bull-fighters,' he explains to Cohn). Yet he
cannot sustain the faith of bullfighting, until the final seg-
ment of the book, when he correctly interprets and imple-
ments it.

 The bullfight and Jake's subsequent trip to San Sebastian
initiate the process of recovery which restores Jake to manhood. These events also release Jake's creative powers and
enable him to become the author of a story which is emotionally valid without being psychologically obsessed. In this
story, author, narrator, and protagonist enjoy a unity of
voice and purpose which, like the oneness of Romero, the
bull, and Brett, images the unifying power of art itself. Jake
is only a spectator at the bullfights, a reader of the text. In
San Sebastian, however, he is actor and interpreter both. His

swim at San Sebastian is not just a ritual immersion. It is a vital confrontation with sexuality and with death. Diving down to the 'green and dark' bottom of the ocean, eyes open—in contrast to his drunken 'blindness' and his being 'blind' to his feelings about Robert Cohn, and to Cohn's near-sightedness—'trying to swim through the rollers, but having to dive sometimes,' Jake swims 'slowly' and 'steadily.' Like Romero, Jake consents with his body, deliberately exulting in a physical pleasure that is an undifferentiated sexuality, even an autoeroticism (one might feel here the pressure of Walt Whitman's sensuous description of the twenty-eight male bathers in 'Song of Myself,' in which the males are each alone and separate, yet all together, and united also with an unseen female presence). Yet, like Romero in the bullfight, controlling the 'locality' of the fight, Jake controls both his swim and the sexual overflow of his text. Like the bullfight, the swim and the telling of it are strong enough, self-confident enough, to reclaim and legitimize even the possibility of male love which in chapter 3 had occasioned the flight into the repressive denial and sterility that led to the frozen and impotent statue of Ney and to the stalled text of the early portions of the book. The account of the swim celebrates the solitary confrontation between a man and himself, a man and his death, in which, mounting the threat of his own weakness and possible destruction, Jake, like Romero, comes clear.

Earlier in the novel Jake had described the 'smooth waves' of his mind which had pushed him towards emotional cleansing. In book I Jake's emotions culminated in tears. Now he not only controls his catharsis, he converts it into usable knowledge and an artistic moment. Twice repeated, like Romero's two separate bullfights, and like Romero's self-awareness and self-control *vis-à-vis* Brett, Jake's two swims and his accounts of them represent the difference between raw experience and self-referential, self-knowing, and self-controlled experience, the difference between Jake's autobiographical text and the living commentary on that text which becomes a new text. Earlier the many repetitions and doublings had represented blind re-enactments. In book III repetition comes to signal the same possibility for meaning's own increment that the Old Testament repetitions represented. Whereas Jake was once a puppet playing out a pantomime directed by Brett, jerking back mindlessly to Brett's every pull of the threads that bind them (as did the toy boxers on strings), now he directs the action, as his telegram to Brett and their subsequent conversation reveal.

Jake emerging from the waves is purged of Cohn, of Romero, and of the ghosts of self-doubt and wish-fulfilment that have haunted his life and his text. His doubles have been banished. He is his own man. What he does at the end of the novel he does for himself. When Brett's telegram arrives, also twice, Jake is ready and able to respond. More important, he is ready and able to acknowledge the meaning of his response, to respond, as it were, also twice:

> LADY ASHLEY HOTEL MONTANA MADRID ARRIVING SUD EXPRESS TO-MORROW LOVE JAKE

> That seemed to handle it. That was it. Send a girl off with one man. Introduce her to another to go off with. Now go and bring her back. And sign the wire with love. That was it all right. I went in to lunch.

THE SUN RISES FOR ONE AND ALL

The post–San Sebastian Jake, like his earlier self, signs his telegram with love and goes in to lunch. He repeats himself, as he repeats Cohn and Romero. But his words do not mean what they seem to mean, and the voice which clarifies the complexity of Jake's language is not Hemingway's or a distorted echo of one of Jake's doubles, but his own. This is repetition not as *déjà vu* or repression or projection, but as self-knowledge and self-control. Jake's commentary on his own telegram changes our reading of it. The telegram thus rendered is not mushy and naive. It is tense, controlled, even bitter. It is, like Hemingway's novel, text and necessitated commentary both. Jake may never be wholly free of the Robert Cohn part of himself that signs his telegram with 'LOVE.' But he can now acknowledge that part of self and deal with it.

In the final moment of the book, Jake, in his own voice, frames and analyses the neurotic denial mechanisms which have been operative in much of his earlier text: "'Oh, Jake," Brett said, "we could have had such a damned good time together." . . . "Yes," I said. "Isn't it pretty to think so?"'

Though it is Romero who has technically 'ruined' Cohn and 'wiped [him] out,' it is Jake who has effectively eliminated him from his consciousness and hence from the novel. By acknowledging the inevitability of projection and fantasy,

Jake converts the image of Romero from that of a paralysing projection, such as Cohn had been and as Romero too could become were Jake to fixate on him, into a usable one, a projection that readies the self for action. The bulk of the pages remaining after Jake leaves Spain are remarkably free of any projections of self, as Jake proceeds to the independence of mind and voice that denotes the artist and not the patient. The final image of the book, which is neatly inserted between Brett's fantasizing that 'we could have had such a damned good time together' and Jake's penetrating irony, 'Isn't it pretty to think so?,' represents one final, fleeting image of self which, unlike the earlier projections, does not subjugate and debilitate Jake's consciousness: 'Ahead was a mounted policeman in khaki directing traffic. He raised his baton. The car slowed suddenly pressing Brett against me." At the final moment, as Jake and Brett all too easily settle back into their relationship of make-believe lovers ('We sat close against each other. I put my arm around her and she rested against me comfortably'), Jake retrieves an image of himself in which he is able to assert authority and control, both physically and psychologically. As Romero was able to mount the bull, and Jake was able to mount the waves, so Jake is also able to mount the emotions and complexities of his relationship to Brett. The policeman 'mounted' on a horse summons up an image similar to that of Romero conjoined with the bull. His raised baton, like Romero's sword, images psychosexual power, aggression, self-defence, and consolidated maleness. An instrument of authority, control, even potential violence, it facilitates rather than destroys the possibility for love: 'The car slowed suddenly pressing Brett against me,' Jake reports. The rhythm it orchestrates is totally unlike that of the drummer and his compulsive, meaningless '. . . . . .' It slows the car (Romero fights slowly, Jake swims slowly, Hemingway's text unfolds slowly), allowing Jake to regain his composure and pronounce the book's final, measured words: 'Isn't it pretty to think so?' In their terse restraint, their self-composed power, and their self-awareness, these words represent Jake's triumph as a man and as a writer.

Through a large portion of the novel, Jake's narration has been a fantasy, a projection of the qualities he would like to have had, and yet a nightmare rendering of the story which is his life. At the beginning of the novel Jake is an inattentive reader of texts—of the texts of others and of himself. By the end, however, he has become the kind of artist-critic which his author has been all along. *The Sun Also Rises* is not simply a story about a lost generation, but about how a lost generation may find itself, how the sun may rise again, for both an individual and for his generation. The Jake who had begun his novel with the language of adolescent rage concludes it with a commentary which is Hemingway's as well as his own.

Narration in *The Sun Also Rises*

Terrence Doody

In this selection, Terrence Doody examines the dichotomy between Jake Barnes, the fictitious "author" of the novel, and Hemingway, who is pulling the strings. Jake artfully breaks character more than once to make a point of Hemingway's, but the fact that Jake himself is supposed to be an impersonal observer by nature makes his having purportedly written a novel about his emotional nadir a bit of a paradox. Terrence Doody is a professor of English at Rice University. His publications include Confession and Community in the Novel *and* Among Other Things: A Description of the Novel.

> In the morning it was raining. A fog had come over the mountains from the sea. You could not see the tops of the mountains. The plateau was dull and gloomy, and the shapes of the trees and houses were changed. I walked out beyond the town to look at the weather. The bad weather was coming in over the mountains from the sea.

With its insistent observation, simplicity, and repetitions this paragraph, which opens Chapter XVI of *The Sun Also Rises,* is a quintessential example of Hemingway's style, which we have honored because it has worked so well to recover for us (in Merleau-Ponty's phrase) "a naive contact with the world." Despite its naivete, however, Hemingway's style is not simply simple. And this paragraph of description is also a paragraph defining character. For it proceeds from the mouth of Jake Barnes, the novel's narrator, who makes it not because he is interested in giving a weather bulletin; but because at this point in the chaos of the fiesta at Pamplona, the weather is a certainty and getting it exactly gives Jake something, however incidental, to hold on to. It is an arresting paragraph because, as Edwin Muir says, Hemingway's power of "observa-

Excerpted from "Hemingway's Style and Jake's Narration," by Terrence Doody, *The Journal of Narrative Technique,* vol. 4, no. 3 (September 1974). Reprinted with permission.

tion is so exact that it has the effect of imagination." For Hemingway, observation is an imaginative act, the issue of his style; but for Jake, who does not have "a style," it is something else. And this discrepancy is what raises problems about Jake's act of narration. . . .

WHEN AND WHY IS JAKE "WRITING" THE NOVEL?

All first person narratives require of the reader a certain suspension of disbelief, the willingness to overlook such matters as the narrator's perfect total recall. . . . But the reader can legitimately ask for some indication that the narrator knows what he is doing and why he is doing it. If Jake were simply a passive behavioralistic register, there would be no problem; for then we could resign ourselves to seeing him as the medium through which events are made manifest and read *The Sun Also Rises* as something other than the novel of education that it is. Or if Jake were more completely dramatized in time, there would be no problem with the conclusions he draws in the paragraph about Bocanegra. But Hemingway wants it both ways. In order to preserve the famous immediacy, Hemingway cannot acknowledge that Jake's different perceptions have different styles of expression, which originate in Jake and for which he should have the authority. In other words, the prose changes, but Jake is not allowed to change it himself or see himself as changing. Time is denied, in effect, and with that denial Hemingway deprives Jake of both his freedom and his autonomy.

Jake seems to be at his most behavioralistic when he describes the Spanish street dancers in Chapter XV.

> In front of us on a clear part of the street a company of boys were dancing. The steps were very intricate and their faces were intent and concentrated. They all looked down while they danced. Their rope-soled shoes tapped and spatted on the pavement. The toes touched. The heels touched. The balls of the feet touched. Then the music broke wildly and the step was finished and they were all dancing up the street.

The dancers' gaze directs Jake's; responding to them first, he then sees and appropriates their dance, the music that orders it, and their career the street. Though Jake does not give meaning to this dance in the way that he gives meaning to the weather, his response is not simply determined by it. No one else in the novel has the intensity of perception that allows Jake to see this dance so clearly; and in fact, his description of the dance comes in answer to Bill Gorton's un-satisfying generalization that "They dance differently to all the different tunes."

JAKE "WRITES" OTHERS BETTER

Jake's ability to see into the nature of things and to inform these things with his own values becomes even more apparent during the bullfights, which are at the center of the novel's meaning. Though he is no longer an able Catholic, Jake is an *aficionado* who has been confirmed by a laying on of hands, and he can see in the bullfights what most of the native Spanish spectators cannot: Belmonte's arrogant, classical integrity and Romero's act of romantic transformation. When he comes to describe Belmonte, Jake's paragraphs grow noticeably longer, and his narration is more fluent than it is anywhere else in the story. This next paragraph could not be more different than it is from the earlier stream-of-consciousness paragraph when Jake tries to pray in the Pamplona cathedral. The two paragraphs are exact thematic counterparts: Jake has difficulty praying, but no trouble at all in seeing the ritual that Belmonte both enacts and defies.

> Also Belmonte imposed conditions and insisted that his bulls should not be too large, nor too dangerously armed with horns, and so the element that was necessary to give the sensation of tragedy was not there, and the public, who wanted three times as much from Belmonte, who was sick with a fistula, as Belmonte had ever been able to give, felt defrauded and cheated, and Belmonte's jaw came further out in contempt, and his face turned yellower, and he moved with greater difficulty as his pain increased, and finally the crowd were actively against him, and he was utterly contemptuous and indifferent. He had meant to have a great afternoon, and instead it was an afternoon of sneers, shouted insults, and finally a volley of cushions and pieces of bread and vegetables, thrown down at him in the plaza where he had had his greatest triumphs. His jaw only went further out. Sometimes he turned to smile that toothed, long-jawed, lipless smile when he was called something particularly insulting, and always the pain that any movement produced grew stronger and stronger, until finally his yellow face was parchment color, and after his second bull was dead and the throwing of bread and cushions was over, after he had saluted the President with the same wolf-jawed smile and contemptuous eyes, and handed his sword over the barrera to be wiped, and put back in its case, he passed through into the callejon and leaned on the barrera below us, his head on his arms, not seeing, not

hearing anything, only going through his pain. When he looked up, finally, he asked for a drink of water. He swallowed a little, rinsed his mouth, spat the water, took his cape, and went back into the ring.

The long sustained lines of this paragraph are Jake's tribute to Belmonte's endurance and as firm in their expression as Belmonte is in his. But because Romero is doing something quite different in converting his bullfight into an act of tribute to Brett, Jake's description of him is appropriately different.

> Pedro Romero had the greatness. He loved bull-fighting, and I think he loved the bulls, and I think he loved Brett. Everything of which he could control the locality he did in front of her all that afternoon. Never once did he look up. He made it stronger that way, and did it for himself, too, as well as for her. Because he did not look up to ask if it pleased he did it all for himself inside, and it strengthened him, and yet he did it for her, too. But he did not do it for her at any loss to himself. He gained by it all through the afternoon.

Jake is both uncertain and insistent here. The hesitancy and repetition of these sentences, the parallels of contrast, express and enforce the tension between Romero's discipline and his aspiration, between what he is doing in conformity with the rite and what he is doing beyond that as an offering to Brett. And we can feel Jake working as hard as Romero does to understand exactly what Romero is doing. Although he loves Brett desperately, Jake re-creates Romero's gift and makes its creation understood with a generosity even more impressive than his ability to see it in the first place. . . .

JAKE'S UNSELFCONSCIOUSNESS OCCASIONALLY CRACKS

Jake is only self-conscious enough to be suspicious of "all frank and simple people, especially when their stories hold together" and to be worried about how fair he is being to Cohn, whom he initially likes in spite of everything. These signs—and there are others like them—are fairly unexceptional notations of Jake's credibility, and they all come early in the novel, in Paris, long before Jake is required to face the bullfights. Moreover, Cohn is much less important as the test of Jake's honesty than he is as Jake's antagonist and antitype. In *The Sun Also Rises,* Cohn absorbs much of the self-indulgence and sentimentality that later afflicts, and consecrates, so many of Hemingway's leading men. And what is most damning about Cohn is that he is a bad novelist, who profiteers on his popularity and who is described by Bill as a "great little confider." Jake, of course, is no confider at all. Only Brett knows his real pain, and only the unspecified reader has any access to Jake's thought. For though he is a writer by profession, Jake neither writes nor tells his narrative to anyone in particular, not even to himself. There is in *The Sun Also Rises* no formal recognition of the motive or the occasion of Jake's retrospect, nor beyond that is there any indication of his imaginative agency in producing the narrative, if even only for the purpose of his own self-discovery. So, we are asked to suspend our disbelief to the extent that we can accept the perfect paragraphs about Belmonte and Romero as coming from right off the top of Jake's head. And we are therefore led to conclude that Jake cannot be self-conscious without violating Hemingway's code. For if he were to solicit an audience, or commit his perceptual experience and moral education to a formal mode, Jake would apparently relinquish the integrity and self-control, with all their noble helplessness, that Cohn relinquishes all the time by being so helpless in public. Art and morality are therefore at odds in *The Sun Also Rises,* and Jake's narrative is left formally suspended in the caesura between the many fine things Jake is supposed to be and the very few things he is allowed to do. Jake himself is left with only the bullfights and his "good behavior" because he does not have the novel he narrates. The only thing we see Jake write is a telegram.

JAKE'S "STYLE" VERSUS HEMINGWAY'S "NARRATION"

Beyond all the familiar questions about Hemingway's indifference to history, culture and the mind, there is still the question of his personal *involvement* in his own art and how this affects the nature of his characters. In the case of Jake Barnes, the first answer to suggest itself is that Jake, despite his general reliability and clear virtue, is a profoundly ironic characterization: a portrait of the artist as an early middle-aged loser. For he has been given formidable powers of perception and a fine sense of language, but is left holding them in a situation that suggests they are insufficient and effete. Though this may be the case in fact, it does not seem to be the novel's intention, and there is nothing else in Hemingway's work or career to support such a reading. For all his other interests in the sporting life, Hemingway speaks of the artist's vocation always with the utmost seriousness; and no one in the twentieth century fashioned a more public and romantic career *as a writer* than Hemingway did.

The second answer is that Hemingway does not realize what he is doing to Jake because he has not thought out the first person novel and its demands with enough care. This reading seems more defensible. Hemingway's most frequent mode of narration is the kind of omniscience he uses to tell the story of Nick Adams in "Big Two-Hearted River." In time and characterization, Nick Adams is close to Jake. Nick's retreat to a pastoral fishing ground and his need for personalized rituals are, like Jake's, the method of his post-war education in the discipline necessary to "live in it" (Jake's phrase). Nick, however, is not the narrator of his story. All of his experience and responses are presented through the intimately omniscient third person that Hemingway uses so well to close the distance between subject and object, reader and character. Nick need not be conscious of all the implications of his experience, nor its shape, because the style—Hemingway's style—does all the work of focus and exclusion necessary to convey the pressure Nick works through and against to achieve his self-possession. The power of "Big Two-Hearted River" results from our awareness that Nick endures his need to not-think with such resolution, and our necessarily distant perspective on his enforced unconsciousness is essential to the poignancy we are made to feel in Nick's self-control.

Because Jake Barnes is the narrator, however, the style of *The Sun Also Rises* is supposedly his style. So, our experience of Jake and, therefore, our expectations of him are different. And immersed in his consciousness, we come to see that Jake's value and significance results precisely from his ability to understand the experience he undergoes. Unlike Nick Adams, Jake is not simply holding on and watching; for during the bullfights, he gives himself away to an experience that fosters in him not only a moral selflessness (which is why he pimps for Brett), but also the aesthetic impersonality that is the fundamental imperative of modernist literature.

CHRONOLOGY

1899

Ernest Miller Hemingway is born in Oak Park, Illinois, on July 21, the second of six children of Clarence Edmunds Hemingway, M.D., and Grace Hall Hemingway, a talented singer and music teacher.

1900

Ernest's father, a devoted outdoorsman, teaches him fishing and hunting and the lessons of nature at the summer cottage Windemere in northern Michigan.

1905

Enters first grade with sister Marcelline, who is a year older.

1913

Attends Oak Park and River Forest High Schools, distinguishing himself as an aspiring journalist/writer.

1917

Graduates from Oak Park High School; rejected by army because of eye injury sustained in boxing; works as cub reporter for the *Kansas City Star.*

1918

Sails to Europe in May as a volunteer ambulance driver for the Italian Red Cross during World War I. Legs severely injured by mortar fragments and heavy machine-gun fire on the Italian front midnight July 8, two weeks before his nineteenth birthday; spends months recuperating in a Milan hospital. His romance with a nurse there, Agnes von Kurowsky, will provide the inspiration for his novel *A Farewell to Arms.*

1919

Hemingway returns to the United States, rejected by Agnes as too young, alienated by his wartime experiences; his parents pester him to go to college or get a job.

1920

His mother banishes him from Windemere shortly after his twenty-first birthday.

1921

Marries Hadley Richardson on September 3. In December, using Sherwood Anderson's written endorsement, becomes the European correspondent for the *Toronto Daily Star* and moves with Hadley to Paris. There he becomes friends with Gertrude Stein, Ezra Pound, Pablo Picasso, and other prominent artists.

1922

Stein reads a fragment of his novel-in-progress and suggests, "Begin over again and concentrate." In December, Hadley takes a train to Lausanne, where he is on assignment, and in transit loses a bag containing the manuscripts of all of Ernest's unpublished fiction.

1923

Goes to Pamplona, Spain, for the bullfights; returns to Toronto in time for the birth of his son John Hadley (Bumby) in October; publishes a limited-edition volume, *Three Stories and Ten Poems.*

1924

In Our Time, thirty-two pages of miniatures, published in Paris; assists Ford Maddox Ford in editing the *Transatlantic Review,* which prints "Indian Camp" and other early stories.

1925

In Our Time, U.S. edition, published by Boni and Liveright, includes fourteen short stories plus the Parisian entries; meets and befriends the slightly older and more established writer F. Scott Fitzgerald.

1926

The Torrents of Spring, a satiric attack on his former mentor Sherwood Anderson, published in May. *The Sun Also Rises* is released in October to mostly glowing reviews. Hemingway is hailed as the defining writer of his "lost" generation.

1927

Divorces Hadley and marries Pauline Pfeiffer, a fashion reporter. Publication of short-story collection *Men Without Women,* which includes "Hills Like White Elephants" and "The Killers."

1928

Moves with Pauline to Key West, Florida, where son Patrick is born. Hemingway's father, beset by health and financial problems, commits suicide. Hemingway has an affair with Martha Gelhorn.

1929

A Farewell to Arms, Hemingway's first commercial success, is published; eighty thousand copies are sold in four months, despite (or possibly abetted by) Boston censorship of the serialized version in *Scribner's* magazine.

1930

Breaks arm in car accident near Billings, Montana, one in a lifelong series of injuries to limbs and head.

1931

Son Gregory Hancock is born.

1932

Death in the Afternoon, a book on bullfighting.

1933

Winner Take Nothing, fourteen stories including "A Clean, Well-Lighted Place." Goes on safari to Africa, the setting for his two long stories "The Snows of Kilimanjaro" and "The Short Happy Life of Frances Macomber" (both published in 1936).

1935

Green Hills of Africa, an account of safari adventures.

1936–1937

Travels to Spain to cover the Spanish civil war for the North American Newspaper Alliance; works on propaganda film *The Spanish Earth;* donates funds to the Loyalist cause; publishes *To Have and Have Not*, three interconnected stories.

1938

The Fifth Column and the First Forty-Nine Stories.

1940

For Whom the Bell Tolls, based on his most recent scrutiny of war, is published; an immediate success, it is his last novel for a decade. Pauline divorces him; he marries Martha Gelhorn, moves with her to Havana, Cuba.

1942

Men at War, a collection of war stories, is published. Outfits his boat, the *Pilar*, to hunt German submarines in the Caribbean.

1942–1945

Covers World War II in Europe as newspaper and magazine correspondent. Observes D day firsthand and attaches himself to the 22nd Regiment, 4th Infantry Division for operations leading to the liberation of Paris and the Battle of Hurtgenwald.

1944

Divorces Martha Gelhorn; marries Mary Welsh.

1950

Across the River and into the Trees, a romance, is published and critically savaged.

1953

Receives Pulitzer Prize for his phenomenally successful novel *The Old Man and the Sea.* Returns to Africa for safari with Mary.

1954

In January, severely injured by two successive plane crashes in Africa, erroneously reported dead. Awarded the Nobel Prize in literature for "forceful and style-making mastery of the art of modern narration."

1959

In declining health, follows the Ordoñez-Dominguin bull-fights and celebrates his sixtieth birthday in Spain.

1960

Moves with Mary to Ketcham, Idaho. His worsening depression leads him to enter the Mayo Clinic.

1961

Undergoes shock treatment for depression; early on the morning of July 2 commits suicide by a gunshot to the head; buried in Sun Valley, Idaho.

1964

A Moveable Feast is published, vivid and occasionally nasty sketches of those Hemingway knew in Paris during the 1920s, including Stein and Fitzgerald.

1970

Islands in the Stream, a semiautobiographical novel about the painter Thomas Hudson and his family.

1972

The Nick Adams Stories, which includes previously unpublished stories and fragments.

1981

Ernest Hemingway: Selected Letters, edited by Carlos Baker.

1985

The Dangerous Summer, an account of the bullfighting rivalry between Ordoñez and Dominguin.

1986

The Garden of Eden, a heavily edited and compressed version of Hemingway's last unfinished manuscript, about love affairs between two women and one man.

1987

The Complete Short Stories of Ernest Hemingway, comprising *The First Forty-Nine Stories* and a number of previously uncollected others.

FOR FURTHER RESEARCH

Carlos Baker, ed., *Hemingway and His Critics: An International Anthology.* New York: Hill and Wang, 1961.

Harold Bloom, ed., *Modern Critical Views: Ernest Hemingway.* New York: Chelsea House, 1985.

Kirk Curnutt, *Ernest Hemingway and the Expatriate Modernist Movement.* New York: Gale Group, 2000.

E.L. Doctorow, *Jack London, Hemingway, and the Constitution.* New York: Random House, 1993.

Scott Donaldson, ed., *The Cambridge Companion to Ernest Hemingway.* Cambridge, England: Cambridge University Press, 1996.

Carl P. Eby, *Hemingway's Fetishism: Psychoanalysis and the Mirror of Manhood.* New York: State University of New York Press, 1999.

Sheldon Norman Grebstein, *Hemingway's Craft.* Carbondale: Southern Illinois University Press, 1973.

James Nagel, ed., *Critical Essays on Ernest Hemingway's* The Sun Also Rises. New York: G.K. Hall, 1995.

Charles M. Oliver, ed., *Ernest Hemingway A to Z.* New York: Checkmark Books, 1999.

John Raeburn, *Fame Became Him: Hemingway as Public Writer.* Bloomington: Indiana University Press, 1984.

Kenneth Rosen, ed., *Hemingway Repossessed.* New York: Praeger, 1994.

Frederic Joseph Svoboda, *Hemingway and* The Sun Also Rises: *The Crafting of a Style.* Lawrence: University Press of Kansas, 1983.

Linda W. Wagner, *Ernest Hemingway: Five Decades of Criticism.* East Lansing: Michigan State University Press, 1974.

Delbert E. Wylder, *Hemingway's Heroes.* Albuquerque: University of New Mexico Press, 1969.

BIOGRAPHIES

John W. Aldridge, *After the Lost Generation.* New York: McGraw-Hill, 1951.

Carlos Baker, *Ernest Hemingway: A Life Story.* New York: Scribner's, 1969.

Anthony Burgess, *Ernest Hemingway and His World.* London: Thames and Hudson, 1978.

Scott Donaldson, *By Force of Will: The Life and Art of Ernest Hemingway.* New York: Viking, 1977.

Charles A. Fenton, *The Apprenticeship of Ernest Hemingway: The Early Years.* New York: Farrar, Straus, and Cudahy, 1954.

Audre Hanneman, *Ernest Hemingway: A Comprehensive Bibliography.* Princeton, NJ: Princeton University Press, 1967.

John K.M. McCaffery, ed., *Ernest Hemingway: The Man and His Work.* Cleveland: World, 1950.

Michael Reynolds, *Hemingway: The Paris Years.* New York: W.W. Norton, 1999.

Earl Rovit, *Ernest Hemingway.* New York: Twayne, 1963.

Linda Wagner-Martin, ed., *A Historical Guide to Ernest Hemingway.* Oxford: Oxford University Press, 2000.

Philip Young, *Ernest Hemingway: A Reconsideration.* University Park: Pennsylvania State University Press, 1966.

WORKS BY ERNEST HEMINGWAY

Three Stories and Ten Poems (1923)

in our time (published privately by a small press in Paris) (1924)

In Our Time (first publication by a major American publisher; includes the stories from *Three Stories and Ten Poems*, the sketches from *in our time*, and new stories) (1925)

The Torrents of Spring; *The Sun Also Rises* (published as *Fiesta* in England) (1926)

Men Without Women (1927)

A Farewell to Arms (1929)

Death in the Afternoon (1932)

Winner Take Nothing (1933)

Green Hills of Africa (1935)

To Have and Have Not (1937)

The Spanish Earth; *The Fifth Column and the First Forty-Nine Stories* (1938)

For Whom the Bell Tolls (1940)

Men at War (edited by Hemingway) (1942)

Across the River and into the Trees (1950)

The Old Man and the Sea (1952)

PUBLISHED POSTHUMOUSLY

The Wild Years (1962)

A Moveable Feast (1964)

By-Line: Ernest Hemingway (1967)

The Fifth Column and Four Stories of the Spanish Civil War (a new edition of the play and four previously uncollected stories) (1969)

Islands in the Stream (1970)

The Nick Adams Stories (includes some previously unpublished Adams material) (1972)

Complete Poems (1979)

Ernest Hemingway: Selected Letters, 1917–1961, edited by Carlos Baker (1981)

The Dangerous Summer; *Dateline: Toronto* (1985)

The Garden of Eden (1986)

INDEX